PRAISE FOR

FIGHT for *JOY*

"In her new book Michele Howe takes you on a magnificent journey of love and healing. Finding joy can sometimes be elusive. As you turn the pages of *Fight for Joy* Michele will be your guide to God's perfect peace as she shares her own struggle to reclaim God's truths for joyful living. This is a must read for anyone who wants to live in God's promises."

— Lucille Williams, Author of *From Me to We* and other titles

"Howe addresses the too-often Christian notion that we will have a life of continuous joy when, in fact, we must fight for it. She shares authentic experiences and reminds us of God's presence in each one. The reminders are perfect for anyone who is going through troubling times. I can think of many times when it would've ministered to me, and I'm sure it will in the future. This book, which is sure to be a Christian classic, ought to be a resource for every counselor and pastor so they can share its wisdom."

— Gail Cawley Showalter, Author of *Living, Learning, Loving: Insights and Encouragement on the Path of Motherhood*

"*Fight For Joy* is a teaching gift to help guide through pain and sorrow, and Michele gives actionable steps based on Biblical principles to motivate and encourage someone who is struggling. I found myself seeking God through the pages and trusting more in Him through disappointments and challenges. I truly feel this book is a great source for steps to take for those who are seeking God more deeply, for the joy and hope there is in Christ."

— Nancy Sabato, host of *The Call with Nancy Sabato*, a weekly Christian talk show

"In her remarkable devotional book, *Fight for Joy*, Michele Howe shares God's Word, her story, and how to fight for joy, whether your life is upended by outer circumstances or a storm of your own making. Each devotional provides help, hope, and a soothing, truth-filled reminder that God is faithful and you are not alone. Whether this book is for you or you're walking alongside someone whose world has imploded, Michele's book will give you a new lens through which to view harsh suffering and hard things, directing you to God's faithfulness, peace, and the cry of your heart for His joy."

— Lenae Bulthuis, Author, Speaker, and Mentor

"When life takes unexpected turns and leaves your heart aching and exhausted, *Fight For Joy* offers a gentle yet profound perspective that our most difficult seasons are opportunities for deep spiritual growth and transformation. This interactive book skillfully guides readers beyond mere survival to see their struggles through the lens of eternity as pathways to holiness and deeper discipleship. Author Michele Howe's compassionate wisdom reminds us that joy isn't the absence of hardship but the gift of God's presence as our Source of strength, help, and hope."

— PeggySue Wells
Award-winning, bestselling author of 45 books, including
Unnatural Cause and *The Ten Best Decisions A Single Mom Can Make*

"Michele Howe, in *Fight for Joy: Discovering Peace in Impossible Circumstances*, reminds us that in life's challenges, obstacles, and even sorrows, we can discover God's true joy. With warmth and wisdom, she guides readers to embrace the hope and confidence that joy is not only possible, but also promised—and abundantly provided by God Himself. In life's darkest moments, the words in this book serve as a lifeline."

— Pam Farrel, author of 60+ books, including the bestselling
Men Are Like Waffles, Women Are Like Spaghetti

Discovering Peace in
Impossible Circumstances

FIGHT
for
JOY

A Devotional by
MICHELE HOWE

Fort Washington, PA 19034

Fight for Joy: Discovering Peace in Impossible Circumstances

Published by CLC Publications

USA: P.O. Box 1449, Fort Washington, PA 19034
www.clcpublications.com

UK: Kingsway CLC Trust
Unit 5, Glendale Avenue, Sandycroft, Flintshire, CH5 2QP
www.equippingthechurch.com

Printed in the United States of America

ISBN (paperback): 978-1-61958-413-6
ISBN (ebook): 978-1-61958-419-8

Italics in Scripture quotations are the emphasis of the author.

To Jim, my husband of over forty years—

Thank you for standing with me, before me, beside me, and behind me, with unconditional love throughout all these years.

Thank you for encouraging me to find my joy in God alone.

Thank you for challenging me to trust in God alone.

Thank you for your stellar example to make God our everything as you lead our home.

And from my mother and grandmother's heart—

I love you, my dear children and grandchildren, more than words can convey.

Each of you lights up my world with blessings incomparable.

Nicole and Jim Zatko
(Logan, Tyler, Jon)

Katlyn and Chase Canning
(Charis, Thea, Simon)

Corinne and Ricky Pratt
(Elias Pratt)

James Howe III

Contents

Acknowledgments

EVERY calendar year includes beginnings and endings, both personally and professionally. I'm in the most contented of professional positions because I have the privilege to be one of the wonderful authors of CLC Publications. Glory be!

Thank you, David Fessenden, editorial director. I am so grateful for your kindness and encouragement as I put down my thoughts on fighting for joy. I send my deepest appreciation and thanks to you and everyone else at CLC Publications, including Jim Pitman, publisher; Jeanette Littleton, editor; Amy Beevers, associate editor; Kaitlin Hakes, marketing; and Marcia Hartman, sales.

Each of you is so uniquely gifted in what you do to create a book that has eternal implications. I marvel at how my sometimes clumsily typed words are transformed into a beautiful product for readers to hold and treasure as I do.

Often when I'm writing I am also praying, "Help! Help! Help!" followed by, "Thank you! Thank you! Thank you!"

Many of those prayers of thanks are extended on behalf of all of you. I am most humbly grateful for each of you at CLC Publications.

I also want to express my kindest appreciation to Bob Hostetler, who represents me at the Steve Laube Agency. Thank you, Bob, for listening to my heart's desires and standing beside me as we work to create another resource worthy of Him.

Introduction

Lord, high and holy, meek and lowly,
Thou has brought me to the valley of vision,
Where I live in the depths but see thee in the heights;
Hemmed in by mountains of sin I behold thy glory.

Let me learn by paradox
That the way down is the way up,
That to be low is to be high,
That the broken heart is the healed heart,
That the contrite spirit is the rejoicing spirit,
That the repenting soul is the victorious soul,
That to have nothing is to possess all,
That to bear the cross is to wear the crown,
That to give is to receive,
That the valley is the place of vision.

Lord, in the daytime stars can be seen from deepest wells,
And the deeper the wells the brighter thy stars shine;
Let me find thy light in my darkness,
Thy life in my death,
Thy joy in my sorrow,
Thy grace in my sin,
Thy riches in my poverty,
Thy glory in my valley.[1]

---

1 Arthur Bennett, *The Valley of Vision* (Carlisle, PA: Banner of Truth Trust, 1975), xxiv–xxv.

IN MY JOURNEY back to joy, I've learned the paradox described throughout this poem from the classic devotional, *The Valley of Vision*, first published over fifty years ago. I've often reread this particular passage because it constantly reminds me that God's way is so very different than my own.

The Lord used the writings of the Puritans to deepen my understanding of Scripture and to strip bare my heart of so many unbiblical misconceptions I've held since my early walk with Christ, which also began over fifty years ago. It's been a journey of discovery and of lament and much-needed introspection as the Holy Spirit revealed the waywardness of my often fickle heart.

As I began writing this book, my heart was in the throes of healing from an especially difficult year of losses and personal weariness. God used every loss to draw me nearer to Him. God used my soul exhaustion and grief to shine His light deeply into my heart as He revealed areas He wanted to cleanse and purify. Praise Him!

This time of journeying back to joy has been one of the most painful, yet joyful, periods of my life. Like so many seasons that are filled to overflowing with hardship, grief, and sorrow (seasons none of us would ever want to repeat) but in the same vein we wouldn't trade them either; my response is, "But God."

Because of the good work God is doing (and has done) in our lives, we know Him more intimately. We trust Him more fully. We worship Him more completely. And our joy is fuller and more abundant because of the trials we have endured.

No, I wouldn't want to retread my steps of the past year, but I am deeply grateful for the good that God has brought because of my pain.

God is good. God does good. That's all we really need to know.

My prayer for you, dear reader, is this: Read through this devotional slowly and take time to reflect upon each chapter's biblical principle. This journey to joy cannot be hurried or rushed.

But it can certainly change us from the inside out as we take time to ponder the grandeur and glory of our heavenly Father in the midst of our travail and suffering.

Just as grief and sorrow do not have an expiration date, do not attempt to rush through your own season of lament. But do take heart that our beloved heavenly Father has promised to stay by our sides and walk us through our shadow days until we emerge stronger, more resilient, and with a joy that cannot be diminished, even by impossible circumstances.

God does good. God is good. That's all we need to know. Truly.

1

Joy: Not Only Possible, But Also Promised

You make known to me the path of life;
you will fill me with joy in your presence,
with eternal pleasures at your right hand.

Psalm 16:11

In the last year, our family made the heart-wrenching move from our church home of eighteen years to a new church fellowship; our beloved nephew took his own life; I was handed a cancer diagnosis, along with several potentially debilitating physical diagnoses; our four adult children (and their families) battled their own uniquely difficult seasons with unstable work situations and complicated, lingering illnesses; and my elderly parents face hardships (physical and mental) in quicker succession than ever before.

If these life-altering situations weren't enough to send my joy meter plummeting (and they did), each of my dearest friends faced their own overwhelming array of life's giant foes. No wonder that I felt joy-less most of the time.

Instead of basking in God's good grace and experiencing that long-forgotten, joyful feeling of peace, I was undone emotionally and otherwise. Tears were a constant companion. Worry pressed in on me during the long, sleepless night hours. I was too well acquainted with fear and anxiety.

In truth, I was coming apart at the seams, even though I was dutifully continuing to do all the right things: read my Bible, pray, memorize passages, and meditate on key verses. Still, my heart was in tatters.

If, like me, you've been in such circumstances or similar seasons when your life feels like it has been upended on every side, then you personally know we face times in our lives when we have to *fight for joy*.

This has been one of those seasons for me and our family. During this year of multiple losses I've learned this: I can take the Lord at His Word and believe Him when He says, "You will fill me with joy in your presence" (Acts 2:28). Or I can continue to live paralyzed by my ever-changing, fickle, dark emotions. I have a choice and so do you.

As I discovered during my journey through grief and sorrow, I realized something that eventually helped me take stock of my habitual dismal outlook. I had forgotten the power of immersing myself daily (sometimes many times each day) in God's promises.

While I had read these precious promises many times, I neglected to take the time to let their truths penetrate my deeply hurting heart. Just as I wouldn't treat a broken limb with a bandage, I've learned that I need more than a surface reading of God's living Word to sustain, strengthen, and heal me. I need to be immersed in the Word. I need to settle long in His presence.

In Hebrews 4:12, we read, "For the word of God is alive and active. Sharper than any double-edged sword, it penetrates even to dividing soul and spirit, joints and marrow; it judges the thoughts and attitudes of the heart."

This familiar passage awakened in me a new revelation, a fresh hope, and a promise for enduring joy. I realized that a cursory reading of God's Word isn't enough when our hearts are breaking. No, what I needed was a deep dive into the mystery and mercies of God's love toward His children. I required spiritual heart surgery.

And I believe this is what God wanted too. So, ever so slowly, I attempted a jump-start of sorts in my journey back to joy. I started to *fight for joy*. I began to linger longer in those specific passages that spoke hope to my heart. I allowed myself long stretches of time to simply sit in silence before the Lord begging Him to help me, encourage me, and reorient my thinking so that I could view all these painful losses from another (better and eternal) perspective.

Each time my thoughts started taking me down the dark tunnel of depression, I stopped myself. I prayed out loud, asking the Lord to give me the strength and grace to trust Him more deeply with these hard and confusing circumstances. I also began to discipline myself to say, "Thank you, Lord," for what He allowed. Honestly, I finally understood what it means to offer a "sacrifice of praise," during these heartbreaking moments.

I knew I needed to reframe all the hurt I endured, the helplessness I battled, into a hopeful, joyful, very present possibility that God was doing a good work in me through this season of sorrow.

I wish I could say I suddenly felt all better and my joy abounded, but that isn't what happened. In fact, I'm still fighting for joy on some days. But God has begun to transform my sorrowful, defeated heart into something sturdier and more resilient, and something that images Jesus more closely. Joy is not only possible, it is promised. But the hard truth is: Sometimes we have to *fight for joy*.

My Heart's Cry

Father, I focus so much on finding relief from pain and suffering that I forget my greatest need is always a spiritual one. You are my Savior, my Sustainer, and the only One who fills my heart with joy. As I look to You for grace and strength to endure this hard season, I face the truth that You have promised to make known the paths of life to me. As I sit in Your holy presence, there alone with You, I find joy. What a precious promise this is to me in this hard season.

Fighting for Joy

1. *Find joy in God's past faithfulness.* Take a look back and thank God for the how He lovingly met your needs when you felt sorrow, grief, and pain. Write a few of these memories in your journal to remind yourself of His uniquely designed, loving care for you.
2. *Find joy in God's present faithfulness.* Today, take time to reflect on any worries or fears you may battle. Ask God to help you to trust Him with every concern great or small. As you pray, remind yourself of God's promises to never leave or forsake you.
3. *Find joy in God's future faithfulness.* Spend time alone with God this week in silence, asking Him to renew your weary heart with His abundant joy. Then give thanks for the eternal truth that God takes the impossible and makes it possible for our good and His glory.

2

Peace that Thrives in Impossible Circumstances

***Peace I leave with you; my peace I give you.
I do not give to you as the world gives. Do not
let your hearts be troubled and do not be afraid.***

John 14:27

ONE TRUTH I discovered in my journey back to joy was this: When your world implodes piece by piece, you soon have another foe to battle beyond trying to rebuild your life. That enemy is fear.

When we are on the receiving end of sorrow upon sorrow, loss upon loss, much we counted on for stability and normality vanishes. As those significant grief-producing losses take their toll, we often forfeit our inner peace. It's almost as if a series of heart-breaking circumstances is set in motion, and we begin to feel layer upon layer of collateral damage to our heart—and waves of fear settle in to take permanent residence.

After weeks of heart-wrenching grief, I began asking myself, "When will the losses stop?" It felt as though each week (if not every day) brought another significant loss.

Leaving a church meant losses in dear friendships. Loss of our nephew meant a sorrow that continued indefinitely. Loss of health means adopting different lifestyle habits to offset persistent illness.

The loss of all of these often-taken-for-granted means of security required rethinking, readjusting, replanting, and starting over . . . again and again. And what is harder during these times is that we feel anything but strong, energetic, and robust enough to handle these demanding life restarts.

These challenging circumstances of suffering and grief change us forever. But the beauty of this crossroad juncture in our lives is this: No matter what our circumstances, our losses, the depth of our personal sorrow—we can experience inner peace even when "things" don't get better or turn out as we hoped.

God tells us that He will give us something so much worthier than simply easing our troubles away. Indeed, He promises us a peace so supernaturally bestowed that any earthly remedy or treasure pales in comparison.

We read this promise in John, "Peace I leave with you; my peace I give you. I do not give to you as the world gives. Do not let your hearts be troubled and do not be afraid."

Even while we feel mired in pain, God tells us we can experience inner peace. Despite the impossible situations we may face, we do not have to be troubled or afraid. Though we feel weak, weary, and depleted, God says we can have a peace that reaches beyond the borders of our troubles and transforms our hearts—and in time, our very lives.

As we allow this precious truth to permeate our hearts, our minds, our souls, we can move from a place of fear and trembling to one of peace and joy. Rather than our living paralyzed in our emotional pain, God gives us what we need to move to a place where we are thriving.

Yes, we can journey from our prison of temporal suffering and discomfort to one where we gaze upon God's glory in the midst of surrounding darkness. His light shines on. His love gives us new life both for today and throughout eternity. His presence offers us comfort, security, and the ultimate stability our hearts crave.

It's true. We can experience peace deep within our hearts even in impossible circumstances. God promises, and we can receive.

So, when that next wave of anxiety hits hard, and we are tempted to retreat into defeat and inaction, we can cease striving and run to the Father. We can tune out the demands of the day, turn off the enemy's voices in our minds, and turn to Him in prayer, in praise, and in thanksgiving. God promises peace, and God does not lie.

My Heart's Cry

Father, today is one of those days when I feel so weary from the trials we are going through that I fear I don't have the strength to press on. I feel paralyzed by all that I have lost. Help me, Lord, to believe Your promise to give me a supernatural peace that doesn't depend on good circumstances. Bless me with an increasingly stronger faith so that I trust in Your plan even when I don't understand it. Thank You, Lord, for giving me what the world cannot give—Your peace. I receive it gladly. Amen.

Fighting for Joy

1. *Find joy in God's past faithfulness.* Spend time reflecting on seasons when you felt uncertain and afraid about events in your life. Ask God to help you remember how He rescued you, how He resolved hard issues, and how He transformed these difficulties into something beautiful to behold.
2. *Find joy in God's present faithfulness.* Lamentations 3:22–23 (ESV) promises that God's mercies are new every morning. Today ask God to show you His new-morning mercies with

spiritual eyes that truly see His gifts, His goodness, and His grace for today. Thank Him for these reminders of His persistent love toward you even when life is hard and the way is unclear.

3. *Find joy in God's future faithfulness.* Before you begin your day, ask God to calm any fears, settle any worries, and take away any anxiety about the future. Ask Him to fill your heart with His perfect peace, and then thank Him for the good work He is doing in your heart and life. Bless the Lord with praise and thanksgiving because you know the God you serve is worthy of your trust, even when life hurts.

3

Contentment Even in Sorrow

But godliness with contentment is great gain, for we brought nothing into the world, and we cannot take anything out of the world.

First Timothy 6:6–7, ESV

I HAVE BEEN leading a small group of ladies in Bible study and through biblical counseling books for fifteen-plus years. During these weekly gatherings, we unpack biblical principles chapter by chapter and precept upon precept. Truly, I am confident that I get more out of these studies than any of the women in my group. I treasure my time spent wrestling through difficult topics as we encourage and exhort one another to trust God and obey Him.

One of the more difficult aspects of meeting over the years is the accumulation of sorrowful life experiences we witness in the lives and families of these dear women. Death. Disease. Addiction. Job loss. Suicide. Familial estrangement. Loneliness. Depression. Financial disaster. You name it and one of these women or I have experienced it.

Perhaps one of the most heart-rending and life-altering, current hardship is that one of our number is facing a terminal cancer diagnosis. Our friend first received her cancer diagnosis fourteen years ago, and through the grace of God, she beat this particular cancer. Several years ago, another more virulent cancer emerged in my friend's body, and she has undergone ongoing brutal treatments, hoping to defeat it.

Our friend is a warrior, to be sure. She has defined courage to me in ways I never expected. She never complains about her pain, her weaknesses, or her suffering. Rather, she exhibits a robust faith in God's perfect plan for her life, even while she fights one day at a time to survive this ordeal.

Beyond her courage, I am amazed by the way she has learned to accept this trial that God has allowed. She has learned to be content no matter what comes next. As I listen to her speak, I have seen something beautiful grow within her heart and soul.

My friend has learned through her suffering that God is good, and He can be trusted.

Let's allow that singular and supernaturally bestowed gift to take hold for a moment. Even though she has suffered for years from two types of cancer and brutal treatments, my friend has learned a life-altering lesson. God is good. God does good. God can be trusted.

She is not only learning the eternally precious lesson of living one day at a time, but she is also content to do so. As I listen to her talk, I see how hard she has fought her disease. I also note how hard she has labored to fight for joy in her life in the midst of this newest trial. How tempting it must be to simply give up in despair and give in to overwhelming fear and discouragement.

And yet, her constant and continual refrain is one of determined hope and trust in God. She amazes me with her response of faith and contentment in the face of such daily uncertainty. I'm also convicted and shamed by my own often-opposite response to the hardships that are part of my life.

Yet, as I confess my own failings and lack of contentment, I sense God urging me to delve deeper in my understanding and knowledge of Him, His faithfulness, and His unchanging character so that I, too, might learn that I can be content even in my most sorrowful seasons.

Lest we forget that every event in our lives is first sifted through the hands of our loving heavenly Father, we must know Him well and be confident in His undeniable love for each of us. God is carefully and supremely reigning over this world and every individual in it. He sees every beating heart and is working to refine and purify each one.

As finite beings, we only see in part, thus we understandably can easily grow discouraged, depressed, even embittered toward God when we suffer. I wish it weren't so but if we are honest, we have all found ourselves lost in sorrow over grief and loss at times.

This is why our own fight for joy is not just for our own sake. My friend's battle to live a daily, contented life, even in the midst of battling cancer, benefits us all. Her fight is both public and private. As a sister in the Lord, she has encouraged me time and again, as I witness her example of trust in God. Her words, her life, and her determination to be joyful every day pierces my often-vacillating heart.

May each of us learn contentment, no matter where God has placed us. May each of us learn that we will face seasons when we must fight for joy but that battle is worth our effort—and our all.

My Heart's Cry

Father, help me to see Your goodness in every part of my life. Remind me of Your tender love toward me every day. Never let me grow hardened or distant toward You when I feel the weight of sorrow beginning to overwhelm me.

I know that You are good and that You do good. Keep reminding me of Your faithfulness, Your nearness, Your eternal love for me. I sometimes get so focused on my pain that I forget to draw near to You in prayer and petition. Hear the cry of my heart, O Lord. Let me begin again today to give thanks in all things and to offer You a contented shout of joy that all the world can hear. Amen.

Fighting for Joy

1. *Find joy in God's past faithfulness.* Reflect upon past seasons when you felt discontent and a lack of joy. Be honest and be willing to ask yourself some hard questions about why you were in this joyless place. How might you have acted or reacted differently if you were able to go back and reframe your experience.
2. *Find joy in God's present faithfulness.* Today, think about specific areas of your life in which you are struggling to accept God's present will for you. Ask Him to do a deep dive within your heart to reveal any areas in which you are resistant to accepting what He is allowing in this season, and then ask Him to forgive you, restore you, and grant you fullness of joy.
3. *Find joy in God's future faithfulness.* As you pray about the coming days, be specific in prayer, asking God to enable you to live one day at a time in complete peace, joy, and contentment. Come what may, ask the Lord to fill your heart and mind with His bountiful promises to take care of you, guard you, and supply your every need.

4

Inevitable Setbacks

We are pressed on every side by troubles, but we are not crushed. We are perplexed, but not driven to despair. We are hunted down, but never abandoned by God. We get knocked down, but are not destroyed.

Second Corinthians 4:8–9, NLT

MY ADULT SON taught me how to make sourdough bread during the COVID–19 pandemic. He lives in California, and my husband and I live in Michigan. Still, during that horrific time when businesses were closed and everything that possibly could go remote did so, I learned a few new skills. One was baking bread from a starter.

If you're like my son, you enjoy the challenge and the subtle nuances of making something delicious out of a few simple ingredients. If you're like me, you would rather bake according to defined rules and measurements for the best possible outcome.

I painstakingly learned to bake sourdough bread well enough that my highly skilled son was proud of me. And yet, at times, I still take all the right steps to create another carefully crafted loaf of bread, but it falls flat, and I wonder what I did wrong. I mentally go back and replay my steps to try and discover my mistakes.

This can be so frustrating. In fact, at times I have been tempted to toss my starter in the trash and give up ever trying to make another loaf of bread. But I haven't and I won't, because when I get to this aggravating place I remember what my son taught me.

His words resonate in my ears, "Everyone fails at times. Everyone tries to create that perfect loaf, and it just doesn't come together. It's okay to mess up."

Those words translate well into our fight-for-joy journey, don't they?

Consider this analogy. When we are battling for joy in our lives a whole lot of other stuff going on tempts us to give up, throw in the towel, or simply walk away and accept defeat.

When we experience a setback, a fail, or a fall, we are in the perfect position to learn something important. Have you ever considered that God in His ultimate love and wisdom allows us to feel a lack within our hearts so He can teach us something of eternal value?

It's true. When we experience any type of setback, it hurts. It's discouraging, and we feel tempted to give up. This same principle applies when we are trying regain joy in our hearts. We may have countless good reasons for despairing when life goes sour. And we know we are all one breath away from dire circumstances taking front and center in our lives. But the key is that when God allows our lives (and our joy meters) to plummet, He will use these difficulties to drive us closer to Him.

The Lord wants us to find our joy in Him alone. He desires to free us from the fickle constraints of temporary, earthly pleasures that will never satisfy our soul. God wants us to fight for joy every day of our lives, and He gives us plenty of opportunities to do so.

Just as I was tempted to give up my bread making after a few loaves fell flat, I can be tempted to give up in my fight for joy when life hands me a variety of hardships, difficulties, and setbacks. But this is not the response my heavenly Father expects of me.

Rather, I'm reminded of this passage in Second Corinthians 4:8–9, which says that even though "We are pressed on every side by troubles . . . we are not crushed. We are perplexed, but not driven to despair."

How much plainer could this passage be in reminding us that as part of the human race, we will feel these dark emotions? And yet, God calls us to remember His kindnesses, His faithfulness, and the love He has set upon us for all eternity.

This brief message from Scripture exhorts us to remember that even though troubles and setbacks may surround us, we are not to give up our fight against defeat and despair. Instead, we are to be comforted that "even though" the worst may befall us, we can still find our joy intact *if* our joy is found in God alone.

So today, as we face our setbacks, our failures, our falls, let us do so with the confidence that God can and will walk with us each step of the way until we find our feet again on the path He has for us.

Yes, we will fail. Yes, we will fall. But no setback can lay claim to the eternal joy we have in knowing Jesus Christ as our Lord and Savior. And what a joyous "knowing" this can be!

My Heart's Cry

Father, thank You for Your gentle reminders that even when I feel discouraged because of setbacks in my life, You are the only one who can bring restoration, healing, and rejuvenation. You alone are my joy.

Help me to never entertain giving up or giving in to my emotions when they threaten to paralyze me from fighting for joy. I am so thankful for Your continued presence and nearness to me, especially when I feel weak and vulnerable. Never allow me to forget the words of Nehemiah 8:10, "The joy of the LORD is [my] strength!" Amen.

Fighting for Joy

1. *Find joy in God's past faithfulness.* Spend time remembering the kindnesses that God has brought into your life during some of your toughest seasons. Remind yourself of His goodness to you and how His mercies truly were renewed each day of your trial. If you haven't begun a journal of remembrances, do so today.
2. *Find joy in God's present faithfulness.* Thank the Lord today for the answers to your prayers He hasn't supplied yet. By faith, tell the Lord how much you appreciate His intimate care for you, and demonstrate this gratefulness by telling others of His perfect love and care for you. Spend time today in quiet meditation, prayerfully asking God to renew your hope, stabilize your emotions, and give you the strength you need to press forward.
3. *Find joy in God's future faithfulness.* If you are feeling uncertain about the future, remember that God is near to you and will guide you in your next steps. Remember that life's setbacks are never the end of the story; rather, they are opportunities for growth in grace and wisdom and understanding. Setbacks never tell the whole story—only the Lord knows what good He will bring forth from these trials that will result in a personal revival of joy.

5

Say His Name

And whatever you do, in word or deed, do everything in the name of the Lord Jesus, giving thanks to God the Father through him.

Colossians 3:17, ESV

ONE OF MY closest friends has Meniere's disease, which can cause her to drop to the floor incapacitated by debilitating dizziness. This is accompanied by the feeling that the room is spinning uncontrollably.

As if these horrendous symptoms aren't enough, retching, migraines, and a host of other traumatic bodily side effects can follow that last from minutes to hours to days. My dear friend has one of the most medically health-defying cases around. For years, she and her doctors have been trying not only to find a cure, but to simply find a way for her to cope and live fully. And still she suffers, never knowing when her next extreme vertigo attack may strike.

In the forty-plus years we have been friends, my friend has taught me so much about leaning in close and trusting the Lord in those moments (minutes, hours, days) when her Meniere's hits hard, and she is once again immobilized until it runs its course.

Perhaps one of the most difficult aspects of living with this disease is that it gives no forewarning. One second, she is fine. The next, she is tumbling down and incapacitated. It's sudden. It's uncertain. It's horrific.

And yet, as much as this dear one hates this condition, she has told me time and again how good God has been to her. She humbly recounts His many kindnesses and blessings. Even following one of her most painful attacks, she testifies of God's tender, loving care toward her. She is convinced that God is always doing a good work within her heart and soul and that He is using this malady as one of His primary teaching tools. And she is right—for the Bible tells us this is so.

I'm amazed. I'm humbled. And I realize I've been given an immeasurable gift to have such a stalwart friend who, no matter what, will tell everyone of God's tender mercies toward her. Likewise, she often reminds me of this important truth—no one likes to suffer. No one.

But Old and New Testament Scripture both give us snapshots of those who suffered long and hard with various affliction, losses, and grief—and then emerged with a stronger, more resilient faith. We read in Second Corinthians 1:3–4 (ESV),

> Blessed be the God and Father of our Lord Jesus Christ, the Father of mercies and God of all comfort, who comforts us in all our affliction, so that we may be able to comfort those who are in any affliction, with the comfort with which we ourselves are comforted by God.

Thus, God's Word tells us in no uncertain terms that when we suffer, He will use our pain to ease others' suffering.

So how do we make the most of our tribulations when we grow so weary of the battle that we can hardly lift one foot in front of another? I believe we have to embrace two scriptural principles, as my friend has done, to shore ourselves up as we walk through seasons of suffering and fight for joy.

First, we must learn to live within the confines of this twenty-four hour space. Jesus promised His abundant grace and strength—but only for today. When we peer into our uncertain and often scary, overwhelming tomorrows, we rob ourselves of the peace Jesus promised us today. God promises us grace while we are in the battle—not when we worry ahead of time.

Second, we must learn to be content (joyful, even) amid our trials and tribulations. Yes, Colossians 3:17 tells us we should give thanks to God the Father through Jesus in whatever we do (word and deed). This is where my friend tells me that her joy begins to abound, even though she lives with the uncertainty of another Meniere's attack every day.

When we fall into depression, discouragement, hopelessness, and joylessness, we grow paralyzed in our pain. As we learn to accept our season of suffering, we can take comfort in the spiritual truth that God will use our pain for our good, for others' good, and for His glory.

As we slowly learn to live within this twenty-four hour space and we learn to be content, we can rediscover joy, hope, and peace along the way. My friend frequently reminds me that even though she may never be free from Meniere's disease her heart and soul are not bound by her body's sickness. She can, and does, experience joy that surpasses her physical condition.

We can bank on God's beautiful promises to sustain and strengthen us and then, in turn, use our suffering, our woundedness, and our pain to bring consolation to others. As my friend encourages me in my own suffering, "Say His name . . . Jesus, the name above all names." Say it again and again and again.

My Heart's Cry

Father, help me to run to You when I am in my darkest seasons of suffering and pain. Never let me forget that I can utter Your name even in my weakest, most desperate moments, and You will hear and answer me.

Jesus, the name above all names, simply speaking Your name brings me comfort. Help me to remember even when I feel helpless and hopeless that my situation will change and that my heart and soul can be rich with joy, hope, and peace, even when my physical body is weak and suffering. Amen.

Fighting for Joy

1. *Find joy in God's past faithfulness.* Reflect upon difficult seasons when pain threatened to overtake your joy, hope, and peace—and remember how God met you in your suffering. Write down anything (small or large) He did for you in that season that helped to ease your suffering and reminded you of His tender, fatherly love for you.
2. *Find joy in God's present faithfulness.* Today, spend time alone with the Lord in prayer and ask Him to calm any anxiety you may experience. Ask God to give you joy, hope, and peace that will reign supreme in your heart, no matter what foe you may face. Then say His name—Jesus, the name above all names—again and again and again.
3. *Find joy in God's future faithfulness.* Even if you believe your future is uncertain because of your suffering, remind yourself that God has promised to never leave or forsake you. He has promised He will supply your every need, and that includes supernatural grace to face any and every foe. Spend time searching Scripture for verses that define God's unchanging character and meditate on who God says He is—as you do so, your troubles will diminish as you focus on the greatness of our God.

6

Grace Is Only Good for Today

I sought the Lord, and he answered me;
he delivered me from all my fears.

Psalm 34:4

ONE OF THE most memorable quotations I have seared into my mind is from Pastor John MacArthur: "When we worry, we suffer twice."

MacArthur clarified that when we spend our emotional and mental energy fretting over "What ifs?" we forfeit today's joy. He reminded believers that God promised His children grace only for today. God doesn't supply us with grace today when we worry, fret, and become anxious about tomorrow.

More to the point, when we worry, we actually do suffer twice and without the blessing and benefit of God's supernatural grace and strength to face our challenges. So the question remains: Why do we waste our time, energy, and emotional and mental resources worrying about what we cannot control?

In my own fight-for-joy journey this past year, I noticed that I frequently began traveling down the "what if" road, and one of most troubling mental scenarios I allowed to dominate my mind concerned our elderly parents. I gave in to worry and anxiety as I imagined—and then adopted—a catastrophic mindset.

For example, one of our parents received a diagnosis that wasn't life-threatening but could eventually develop into something more serious. What did I do? I mentally traveled down every conceivable rabbit trail trying to get ahead of the problem by formulating solutions, remedies, and cures for something that hasn't even happened—and may never happen.

When I do this kind of thing, I confuse and overly complicate the present, benign situation by unnecessarily trying to take control of something I cannot control. And, as a result, my joy meter plummets.

When I give in to this sinful pattern of worry—and yes, worry is sin—I sabotage my own success in finding joy that is so settled, so firmly in place, and so securely positioned that not even the direst circumstance can dislodge it.

From talking with other believers, I know I'm not alone in my battle against worry. Worry, fretting, and anxiety over the unknown is perhaps one of the most common struggles we humans face. Let's be honest, everyone is afraid of something.

That said, we must realize that our heavenly Father understands our weaknesses, our frailties, and our tendency toward unbiblical thinking that will—and does—harm us and others. God's solution? We must learn to intentionally focus on who God says He is and what He says He will do for us. The more we set our hearts on knowing God more fully as He is revealed throughout Scripture, the more our hearts can be at ease, despite our unruly, untamed, and troubling circumstances.

The Psalms is one of the best books of the Bible to retreat to when we begin to waver in worry and fear. Psalm 34:4 tells us exactly what we should do when worry raises its ugly head again: "I sought the Lord, and he answered me; / he delivered me from all my fears."

We must determine to seek the Lord first and foremost. We must settle quietly in His presence with the Bible open and let His powerful truths begin transforming our thinking.

This isn't a quick-fix approach to remedy our fear-driven minds. Rather, it is a powerful, spiritual discipline that every believer needs to adopt. The more time and energy we invest in knowing the God we love and serve, the better for us, and the more effective we will grow to be as His Word cleanses and sanctifies us.

We must remember that God tells us to renew our minds daily for the simple reason that we are always fighting a spiritual battle. As we step into the armor God has provided for us, and we sit in His presence meditating on His word, we are far better equipped to face down our worry and fear. Why? Knowing God and trusting in His changeless character will eventually change us as He grows bigger and our problems grow smaller.

We will in time begin to change how we initially respond to devastating news by making faith and trust our default response. And our fight-for-joy journey will grow in direct proportion to the investment we make in knowing God more fully and trusting Him more completely.

Indeed, grace is only available to us in this twenty-four-hour space, but as we learn to live within the confines of today's problems alone, it is enough, and our joy can flourish all day long and worry cannot gain entrance.

My Heart's Cry

Father, You know what I'm struggling with today. I'm fighting against worry and the unknown future that I cannot control. I seem to be losing this battle, and I want to change the way I respond to difficult news.

Help me to remember Your faithfulness to me and to set my heart and mind on knowing You more fully. Remind me that I can trust You to care for me and for everyone I love.

You have promised me grace for today alone and that is enough. Give me a fresh measure of joy, hope, and settled peace today. Amen.

Fighting for Joy

Find joy in God's past faithfulness. With journal in hand, recount those times that you felt overwhelmed by troubling circumstances and write down how God met you in your time of need. Find several Bible verses that brought you comfort and consolation during this time and write these in journal as a memorial stone of God's past faithfulness.

Find joy in God's present faithfulness. Think about anything or any situation that has been preying on your mind. Write down these difficulties and then commit each one to God's care and keeping. Remember to spend a few moments in prayerful reflection of how God has always kept His Word to supply you with grace for today.

Find joy in God's future faithfulness. Take time this week to prayerfully ask God to search your heart and mind to see if you are trusting in Him fully for your future. Ask God to reveal any areas where you are sinfully worrying and to give you the faith you require to live fully in joy and peace—this day and every day.

7

New-Morning Mercies

The steadfast love of the Lord never ceases; his mercies never come to an end; they are new every morning; great is your faithfulness.

Lamentations 3:22–23, ESV

GOD HAS A sense of humor. As I prayed about how to approach this chapter's topic on anticipating new-morning mercies, I knew I wanted to address two separate biblical principles.

First, despite how circumstances may appear at first glance (or after fifty long, hard stares), we only see a fragment while God sees the whole. Because we know from Scripture that God isn't confined by time or space, we can trust that when our lives start to turn upside down—from our human perspective—life is not always as it seems.

Again, we see in part, God sees the whole. Thus, we need to see with eyes of faith and find our peace through complete trust in Him.

Next, I wanted to touch upon the need to learn to reframe our difficulties, our hardships, and our challenging days. This whole business of reframing suffering and trials is essential because by doing so, we begin to see God's hand of redemption and restoration all around us.

As we make intentional choices to reframe our situations—troubling though they may be—through the lens of eternity, everything shifts. No longer are we bound by our temporal pain and grief. Instead, we can develop spiritual eyes to see these painful seasons through God's eyes and from His perspective.

God has a sense of humor. Humans make plans and God laughs.

When I woke up, ready to write about new-morning mercies, I received an urgent call from my sister-in-law, who asked for prayer for her granddaughter who faced medical complications and was being induced to deliver her first baby. We talked and I encouraged her to trust that the Lord would be there with them for every step of the delivery process, and I promised to pray.

Within an hour, I received another urgent call. This time from my father who was frantic because my mother had fallen, could not get up, and appeared going into shock.

I gathered the information, ended the call, and rushed to their home. As I was driving, I realized that I had neglected to be on the lookout for those new-morning mercies because I was so distracted and sidetracked by these urgent, and scary, life scenarios.

I then began to pray, "Lord, You knew what my morning was going to be like before I even opened my eyes today. Help me, even now, to see Your new-morning mercies in the midst of these hard things. Amen."

And He did. By faith, I started thanking God that we live in a country where we can get medical care. I thanked Him for a car that runs even in minus-zero weather. I thanked Him for family that cares, family that supports one another, family that is ready to help when the needs arise. By the time I arrived at my parents' home, I was serenely calm and ready to face whatever God had allowed.

The remainder of my day was spent in the ER while my mom was checked for every possible medical condition. As I sat waiting for the various test results to come back, my thoughts continued along the lines of praying for God to give me eyes to see clearly.

I wanted to discern the opportunities God had placed before me even in this hospital setting. Who could I encourage? Who could I talk to about Jesus? How could I ease someone's burden? I was interested to find that the more I prayed for eyes to see, God answered my prayers.

He nudged me to speak up when our nurse talked about churches and missions trips. He gave me words to lift the technicians as they came and went from the room where my mother was being treated.

Yes, it was a long, tiring day. Yet, I knew God was with me. I knew that He saw me and He saw my mother's needs. He was well aware of the needs of my sister-in-law and her granddaughter in another hospital, too. My joy flourished, even when my circumstances felt hard, exhausting, and uncertain.

Our God is so good to us. He alone can supernaturally transform even the most unexpected and unwanted type of experience into something beautiful. As we learn to daily anticipate God's new-morning mercies, I believe our joy meter will continue to rise. We will start to see these mercies everywhere and all the time.

God, give us eyes to see, hearts to discern, and a mind that focuses solely on Jesus. New-morning mercies. God promises them. It's our task to diligently be on the lookout for each one—every day.

My Heart's Cry

Father, I'm having a difficult start to my day. I feel as though I woke up eager to see all the goodness You have promised by way of Your new-morning mercies, and instead, I have seen nothing but trouble. Help me to reframe these hard events and see Your faithful and redemptive hand in every situation. Open my eyes to see all of life's happenings through the lens of eternity, because it helps me gain a better perspective.

Thank You, Lord, for being so near to me and for demonstrating Your kindness to me each day. Amen.

Fighting for Joy

1. *Find joy in God's past faithfulness.* Before arising, ask the Lord to give you eyes to see all the wondrous ways God has blessed your life with daily new-morning mercies. Ask Him to bring to your remembrance the times that were difficult when He demonstrated His faithful kindness toward you in ways both small and large.
2. *Find joy in God's present faithfulness.* Ask the Lord to help you reframe your current struggles into those which will bring Him glory as you choose to trust Him. Write specific Bible passages that bring you comfort and strength as you meditate upon them. Purpose to memorize one verse per week so you are equipped to fight against the schemes of the enemy when he tempts you to doubt God's perfect provision and love for you.
3. *Find joy in God's future faithfulness.* As you pray about the coming weeks and months, write about your burdens in your journal. After each notation, look up an applicable Bible verse and write it underneath. Pray through these hard issues every day, and take time to let the verses and their powerful truths permeate your heart and mind. As you do, note how your joy increases the more you seek to trust God for every aspect of your life and the lives of those you love.

8

Run to God Again and Again and Again

Even if my father and mother abandon me,
the LORD will hold me close.

Psalm 27:10, NLT

SOME PEOPLE SAY the most excruciating relational pain is caused by those closest to us. One of my dearest friends has been subject to rejection and verbal and physical abuse by her parents since she was a young child.

As an older adult, she is now no longer at the mercy of her elderly parents' anger, rage, and attempts to control her. Though my friend is a child of the King of kings, she still feels the woundedness of being brought up in a home without love.

My friend is married, and she has children and grandchildren, as well as many wonderful friends. And yet the wounds inflicted upon her during childhood and her young adult years continue to raise their ugly heads whenever a new fresh onslaught of verbal abuse is aimed her way.

She tells me that even though she has forgiven her parents for their sinful deeds, sometimes those dark memories take front and center in her hurting soul, and she feels the same emotional devastation she did as a small child.

So what does she do? She runs to God again and again and again. In fact, she has made running to her heavenly Father her default response when old memories—or brand new ones—begin to take hold. Rather than give in to despair and depression over what she has suffered, she pours her heart out to Jesus. She has found her comfort and her joy in God alone.

And this, my friend assures me, is where she has found healing and peace and joy that endures. I'm so thankful my friend has discovered that no matter what she has been subjected to in the past, she can find healing deep within through the Holy Spirit's transforming work in her heart.

When we have endured neglect, abuse, or abandonment, God's Word tells us this, "Even if my father and mother abandon me, / the LORD will hold me close" (Ps. 27:10, NLT). What a powerful promise this is to all of us—but especially to those who have never known the consistent and committed love of a father and mother.

While this potent verse can help to heal even the most broken heart, we must consider another biblical principle. Author and speaker Elizabeth Elliot wrote, "There's God's part and there's my part."

God's part opens our heart and minds to our sinful nature, and He saves us from eternal damnation. Our part is to ask for His forgiveness, forsake our sin, and start living a life that pleases Him. Our part also includes incorporating the spiritual disciplines, which are daily Bible reading and study, prayer and praise, meditation and memorization, and a life of selfless service to our church body and to all those whom God brings into our circle.

My friend tells me that the enemy often attacks her with thoughts of past pain immediately before and after she has to see her parents. Even though my friend has set necessary boundaries with her elderly parents, they continue to try to tear her apart with accusatory words and demeaning comments. Again, what has my beloved friend learned to do in this hard relationship scenario? She runs to God again and again and again. In His presence, as the Scripture promises, she finds "fullness of joy" (Ps. 16:11, ESV). So that is where she runs when her heart starts to hurt.

Lest we mistakenly believe that only the brokenhearted or abused need to run to God again and again and again, that's simply not true. Whether or not we have endured painful hardship as a child or some other form of suffering, we all face foes that will try to dismantle our faith, discourage our commitment to God, and make mockery of the Christian journey through this broken world. No one is immune to such hard treatment and potential rejection and abuse.

Jesus said, "In this world you will have trouble. But take heart! I have overcome the world" (John 16:33). Thus we must take Him at His Word and believe Him when He says that every single one of us will encounter trouble, and we should not be surprised when hardships arrive on our doorstep.

Instead of feeling shocked and dismayed, our default response to any form of hardship should be to run to God again and again and again. He alone can counter the world's evils. He alone offers us peace in His presence. He alone can give us joy that endures even the most heart-rending attacks on us.

Let us learn to run to God again and again and again. Our fight for joy demands it.

My Heart's Cry

Father, today I am once again feeling all the hurt and rejection my family has aimed at me. It is as though I'm sinking under the weight of this heavy burden. Please help me to bear up under it and be healed from this pain. I don't want to think about my past anymore. I'm a new person in Jesus and I know You have made me brand new. I am loved by You.

Thank You for setting me free from the chains of anger and resentment I felt for so many years toward those who hurt me so deeply. Give me the grace I need to pray for their salvation and their well-being. Help me to overcome evil with good. And never let me forget I was once Your enemy before You reached down to rescue me from my sins. I will continue to run to You again and again and again, for You have promised to hold me close. Amen.

Fighting for Joy

1. *Find joy in God's past faithfulness.* With journal in hand, write down any past hurts or pain that continue to plague you. Once you have recorded these painful experiences, counter each one with a specific promise from God to heal your heart. Look for these verses throughout the psalms and read through each psalm, noting how most of these passages begin with pain and suffering but end with the writer finding hope, help, and comfort from the Lord.
2. *Find joy in God's present faithfulness.* Spend time each day this week praying about any past injuries you have suffered from those close to you. Ask the Lord to give you fresh eyes and a heart that sees accurately so you can sincerely pray for those who have hurt you. Make your objective to overcome evil with good through your prayers for these individuals.
3. *Find joy in God's future faithfulness.* As you contemplate the past and present, focus your hope on God and the good work that only He can accomplish through forgiveness, restoration, and renewed hope. Make it your habit to run to God again and again and again whenever old memories rear their heads or when fresh hurts occur. Be sensitive to the changes that start to take place in your heart and mind as you make running to God your default response to hurt. Note how your joy starts to grow and deepen.

9

Baby Steps, Even in Pain

The heart of man plans his way,
but the LORD establishes his steps.

Proverbs 16:9, ESV

I WAS REMINDED this morning of an important principle that thousands of believers have benefited from over the years. Most of us have read this famed Elizabeth Elliot quotation, "Sometimes life is so hard you can only do the next thing."

So . . . do the next thing. Sometimes the next thing is taking out the trash, cleaning the bathroom, feeding the dog, writing a thank-you note, or telling someone you love them.

This principle of "next thing" living is vital when we consider that life is sometimes so hard you can only do the next thing. When we experience that kind of day—or week or month—everything seems overwhelming and unattainable. So what do we do? We get up and do our next thing.

I remember how often this principle helped me as I walked through grief last year. Many days, if left to my "feelings," I would not have accomplished a single thing. Tasks would have gone undone. Responsibilities would have been left by the wayside. Relationships would have gone untended to and unnourished.

But as difficult as it was and as grief-stricken as I felt, I did as Elliot suggested. I got up and did my next thing.

And to my surprise, when those small baby steps of next things began to pile up, I started to tame my unruly emotions, and my days grew brighter. I learned the hard way that the more I allowed myself to ruminate over all of our losses, the more I spiraled downward. Not a good choice. But when I did the opposite, and took baby steps to fulfill my tasks, my responsibilities, and re-engage with others in meaningful ways, I started to heal.

Perhaps this was the turning point in my own fight-for-joy journey. I came to the place where I acknowledged my losses and felt them keenly, but I didn't allow the pain to stop me from my next things.

Throughout Scripture, we read about the mighty men and women of God who faced down their own life-changing losses and sorrows. But what made them noteworthy, for our benefit, was that they acknowledged their pain, but they didn't stop living. They dusted themselves off, broken and weary beyond belief, and they stepped out in faith to do their next things.

This is the key point. We will suffer losses in this broken world. We will experience hurt, rejection, betrayal, disloyalty, fractured relationships, and more.

And yet, God tells us that while we are great at planning our way, He alone establishes our steps. God directs us to do our next thing despite our pain and loss. He promises us the grace and strength to do so. He promises to be near to us. He promises to bring hope, healing, and joy to our hearts as we stay near Him.

Yes, even in our pain, we can take baby steps to become useful to God, to others, and to ourselves. But we need to draw close to our heavenly Father and pour our hearts out before Him, confident that He hears us.

We also must have complete trust in His plan and path for us, even when—from our human perspective—everything seems all wrong. This next-thing principle is so essential for those like me who lost their joy or others who struggle with depression and discouragement, and feel utterly defeated by life.

Even when taking a small, baby step feels overwhelming, we must lean hard onto God and His Word that tells us that His strength is made perfect in our weaknesses. The weaker we feel, the more glorious God's perfect love and grace will work through us. He will indeed get all the glory as we allow His Holy Spirit to fill us, teach us, comfort us, and serve through us.

Yes, even when life is so hard that we can only do the next thing, we can step out in faith and take baby steps to become useful again. Our journey to joy demands that we fight for this, and God's enabling grace and strength fit us for the task.

My Heart's Cry

Father, strengthen my heart today to get up and get busy doing my next thing. Give me Your grace and strength to begin taking baby steps in becoming useful again.

I have been feeling so discouraged and joyless of late. I need to draw closer to You and let Your Holy Spirit give me comfort and teach me how to work through my sorrow.

Your Word tells me that You establish my steps, and I pray that You will give me the wisdom I require to step out and start doing my next things. I am longing to feel Your joy again and I know that I will—in time. Thank You for loving me, for listening to my heart's cries, and for giving me hope for a bright future. Amen.

Fighting for Joy

1. *Find joy in God's past faithfulness.* Today, silently reflect upon God's goodness to you. Recall specific seasons when joy felt absent but God entered the scene and supplied you with fresh hope. Be encouraged by God's history of faithfulness to you, and expect that He will continue to build upon this history of faithfulness for your entire life.
2. *Find joy in God's present faithfulness.* Give thanks today for God's faithfulness toward you in every way you can. Thank Him for giving you tasks to accomplish, for responsibilities you are expected to fulfill, and for relationships you are part of. Ask Him to direct you to your own next thing today. Begin small, but be consistent to take baby steps each day, and then give God thanks for the grace to do so.
3. *Find joy in God's future faithfulness.* Feed upon God's promises that tell of His faithfulness for all generations. Take time to record verses that strengthen and reinforce God's perfect love and will for your life. Then meditate on these passages and allow them to become deeply ingrained in your heart and soul. Remember that life is sometimes so hard that you can only do the next thing—but that is all that God expects . . . small baby steps of faithfulness on your part.

10

Eyes of Wonder and Faith

Lord, you alone are my portion and my cup; you make my lot secure. The boundary lines have fallen for me in pleasant places; surely I have a delightful inheritance.

Psalm 16:5–6

LET'S BEGIN THIS chapter with this statement, "God alone is sufficient for my happiness." Because it is true.

Indeed, as we search through Scripture, we discover that when God describes Himself and His unchanging character, He wants us, His dearly beloved children, to know that because of who He is, we can be at peace—no matter what is happening around us. As we consider our lives and our futures, this can be daunting because none of us has a life untouched by sorrow, pain, and suffering.

And yet, despite our living in our broken and sin-ridden world, God tells us over and over again that He is enough for us. He alone can fulfill and satisfy our souls. He alone can calm us, secure our peace, and elevate our joy.

God alone wants each of us to know who He is so that when troubles arrive, we will run to His arms and stay there until the danger has passed.

As we continue to fight for joy in the midst of difficulties today and our uncertain tomorrows, the more we learn about who God is, and the more restful we will become. In the same way, as we prioritize time spent studying God's Word, and especially those passages that declare Him as . . .

Father—*Abba*
Lord and Master—*Adonai*
The Beginning and End—*Alpha and Omega*
The Ancient of Days—*Attiyq Youm*
Living God—*El Deah*
The Mighty God—*El Gibhor*
The God Who Sees—*El Roi*
God Almighty—*El Shaddai*
The Creator—*Elohim*
God with Us—*Immanuel*
The Lord our Provider—*Jehovah-Jireh*
The Lord Who Sanctifies—*Jehovah-M'Kaddesh*
The Lord our Healer—*Jehovah-Rapha*
The Lord our Shepherd—*Jehovah-Rohi*
The Lord is Peace—*Jehovah-Shalom*
The Lord our Rock—*Jehovah-Tsuri*
Our Dwelling Place—*Ma-on*

As we better understand who He is, we will learn to lay down our burdens at His magnificent feet and leave them there.

Only when we fully trust in our always trustworthy God can we overflow with joy, peace, and happiness. Jesus told us that in our world we will have trouble, but He overcame the world (John 16:33).

Again, when we begin to believe within the deepest recesses of our hearts that we can trust God to meet us where we are and care for our every need, only then can we experience the blessings He promises us—joy, peace, and happiness.

Some people may say that in today's world, believers cannot be happy, yet Scripture often discusses the fusion of peace and joy and happiness. The kind of happiness the Bible talks about isn't the world's finicky definition that relies on positive circumstances and security from harm.

Rather, the Bible offers a far more robust type of "happiness" because it only occurs in those believers who make God their happiness, their portion, and their inheritance. As we love our God with all our hearts, no one and nothing can disturb our inner peace and joy and happiness.

Perhaps the most striking benefit of learning to know God as He is revealed in Scripture is that we can learn to view our future unknown through the eyes of wonder and faith because we know we can trust Him implicitly.

As Psalm 16 tells us, God is our inheritance. As such, everything else pales in comparison to knowing God, being adopted into His family, and being given the promise of life eternal with Him and those who share our love for Him. Yet, despite today's bad news, whether personal or worldwide, we can have peace and joy and happiness if we make God the only desire of our hearts. For He alone, and no other, can and will fulfill and satisfy our souls.

And how do we know if we have made God our treasure? Simply, we obey Him. We love Him. We sacrifice for Him.

What else can we do for our heavenly Father who has given His all for us? Peace. Joy. Happiness. What more can we ask?

My Heart's Cry

Father, I am often afraid of the unknowns in my future. Life feels so uncertain and nothing is ever sure. I know You have promised to meet my every need, and I know You are trustworthy. But I am weak in faith and often scared of what I cannot understand and cannot control.

Help me, Lord, to set my mind and my heart upon You alone. Give me wisdom and understanding beyond what this world gives. Reveal to me any idols of my heart that I have placed above my love and devotion to You.

Fill me with joy in Your presence and make known to me the path You want me to take. You are my inheritance and You are all I need. Amen.

Fighting for Joy

1. *Find joy in God's past faithfulness.* Reflect upon God's work in your life in the past when you felt afraid of outcomes. Remember His goodness to you in ways small and large and write these in your journal. Purpose to remember these each day when you start to feel afraid of the unknown tomorrows.
2. *Find joy in God's present faithfulness.* Spend a few moments praying through what worries you or derails your joy. Ask the Lord to help you to reframe each hardship and to see these difficulties as opportunities to run to Jesus for help, for rescue, and to create in you a more stable, robust faith. Thank Him for His mindful care for you and then walk through the day knowing you never walk alone.
3. *Find joy in God's future faithfulness.* As you contemplate the future, be honest about what frightens or overwhelms you. Then revisit the attributes of God listed in this chapter. As you meditate on the unchanging character qualities of God, note how restful you become. Learn to run directly to God when you are afraid and ask Him to give you peace, joy, and happiness in Him.

11

Remember

I will remember the deeds of the Lord;
yes, I will remember your miracles of long ago.

Psalm 77:11

OUR MEMORIES ARE powerful tools to recall both the good and the bad. Yet, God wants us to place our focus on remembering all that He has done on our behalf.

Yes, our loving heavenly Father wants us, as His dearly beloved children, to learn to remember and to remember well. He also wants us to live with our eyes wide open to what He has done and is doing and will do.

It's all about our focus on God and being able to see with spiritual eyes that can reframe even the most heartbreaking situation into something that is good in light of eternity. And yes, these two principles are easier said than done.

I remember some years ago when one of our daughters began making poor choices that landed her in trouble legally and otherwise. She was just graduating from high school when she decided to see what the world had to offer.

For the next five years, we lived in a state of constant alert always anticipating her next foolish choice—and the accompanying costly repercussions. Some days and nights we didn't know if our daughter was safe—or even alive. We spent many days on our knees praying for her return to us and to the Lord.

As I recall those difficult years, I'm amazed that I can talk about them now as if they had happened to someone else. The pain is gone. The suffering is history. The heartache a very distant memory. Why? Because of who God is and what He has done.

Our daughter's rebellion is nothing new, but it was new to our family of six. Our daughter took a route every parent fears, and she paid a high price for her choices. Some days, weeks, and months we struggled to hope that she would ever turn to Christ, repent, and believe. Yet we continued to cry out to God and beg Him to save her.

Yes, it was a grueling season for us as parents, and yet, as much as we desired for our daughter to change, God was in the business of changing us, too. He was faithfully working in our hearts as much as hers. We praise Him for that.

His goodness to us was manifested in many ways. We were blessed with mature, believing friends who stood with us and supported us in prayer. We had family who shared our burden and offered unfaltering comfort and love. And we felt the nearness of God both day and night. What a Savior!

Eventually, our daughter hit rock bottom. No real friends. No job. No car. No insurance. No future. No hope. No happiness. Nothing but God's beckoning call to come to Him for forgiveness and restoration. And yes, some years later, our daughter did come to Jesus asking for pardon, and her new life in Him began. Praise Him!

One of the most important lessons we learned through those lean years of parenting was that we had to choose what to allow our thoughts to dwell upon. We had to decide if we were going to give in to despair or continue to trust God. We chose the latter. Every day we stormed the doors of heaven and interceded on behalf of our prodigal child. And we were surprised by joy, as C.S. Lewis was so fond of saying. Indeed, God met us in our place of sorrow and sadness, and He gave us love, joy, and peace. What a Savior!

While outsiders would ask how we were holding up, we honestly could attest to God's enabling grace and strength that gave us exactly what we needed each day. It was a supernatural outpouring of His love to two weak, frail, and frightened parents. We still talk about God's enduring love toward us and our daughter during those hard years. And we won't forget what He did for us and for her.

In moments when our lives feel like they are falling apart, we must take the same stance as the psalmist and choose to remember the deeds of the Lord and what He has done for us. As we learn to be good rememberers, God will infuse within us a buoyant spirit filled with love, joy, and peace. As we learn to reframe even our most difficult battles into something worthy in eternity, God will open our eyes to see that what He is doing is good because He is good. What a Savior!

My Heart's Cry

Father, I'm feeling overwhelmed by the circumstances in my life today. I cannot change them. I cannot fix them. I cannot find anything good about them.

Please help me to keep my focus on You alone. And please help me to trust that You are accomplishing something good in this season even though I cannot see it. Help me to remember that You are good and all that You do is good.

Lord, I need Your grace, Your strength, and Your divine wisdom to walk through this trial in a way that will bring You glory and honor. Help me now. Amen.

Fighting for Joy

1. *Find joy in God's past faithfulness.* As you begin your day, take time to praise the Lord for His past goodness to you. Remember His acts of compassion and kindness toward you and those you love. Thank Him for His new-morning mercies, even in the midst of hardship and uncertainty. Then ask Him to help you become a good rememberer each day of your life.
2. *Find joy in God's present faithfulness.* Today, recount in your heart and mind every act of goodness that God has bestowed upon you. Despite the struggles and trials you are facing today, thank God by faith that He will do good and redeem every situation into something beautiful in His time. Ask God for eyes to see every trial in light of eternity.
3. *Find joy in God's future faithfulness.* As you pray about the coming days and months, ask the Lord to fill your heart with love, joy, and peace. Ask Him to settle your heart and calm any worries or fears. Do not give way to those sinful thoughts that continually spiral into discouragement, despair, and depression. Call to your mind all that God is and all that He has done—and praise Him continually.

12

Joy in Lament

For we do not have a high priest who is unable to sympathize with our weaknesses, but one who in every respect has been tempted as we are, yet without sin.

Hebrews 4:15, ESV

ONE OF THE most valuable tools in our spiritual toolbox as we battle a joyless spirit is to know to whom we can run to for support, encouragement, and sound biblical counsel. Namely, if we are in close connection with mature believing friends, we can know joy because of them.

How so? The Bible clearly reveals that bad company corrupts good morals, and the opposite is true as well. Sound, mature, godly friends can help us as we fight for joy in our darkest hours.

When I was at my lowest point emotionally after my first of six shoulder surgeries, I became depressed. This was a new low for me, but the depression shouldn't have surprised me when it happened.

My husband and I had been deeply entrenched in caregiving roles for five years; we had four active teens and other complicated life responsibilities we were expected to fulfill. So when I began to recover from my shoulder surgery and couldn't sleep for six weeks, my body rebelled and said, "No more."

I cannot recall another season of life when my emotions were such a jumble of highs, lows, and nothingness than during this time. I remember sitting outside on the grass with my shoulder in a sling, trying to read my Bible to gain fresh hope, joy, and a more positive outlook—but I couldn't. I had been a believer for many years and still I felt undone and utterly discouraged.

One sunny afternoon, after I cried yet again for no apparent reason, a dear friend drove into our driveway and met me with arms wide open. She said, "I felt like a magnet was pulling me to come and see you. I couldn't stay away."

As she hugged me close, I cried yet again. But her embrace —both the words and physical touch—reignited something in me that God used to jump-start my journey back to joy.

We spent a long time talking and praying, and while my emotions didn't really feel any different after her visit, I knew something had changed. Somehow, God used my dear, godly friend to help me unpack my lament, and my weary heart was able to release all the hurt I had clung to. While it would have been wonderful to say to that I said goodbye to my friend, and I felt like myself again, that's not what happened.

What did transpire was this—she helped me to mentally work through my exhaustion and sorrow, and she offered me hope because she had been where I was years earlier. She understood my pain, and I knew it.

In fact, I took great comfort in the fact that someone besides the Lord, someone with skin on, understood what I was going through. And yes, months passed before I regained my physical, mental, emotional, and spiritual equilibrium. But it did return. Thank the Lord.

That year of sorrow, as I later dubbed it, changed me forever. It taught me that even when we do our best to make wise decisions in obedience to God, this life can be immeasurably hard and heartbreaking. I also learned that I have a High Priest who is able to sympathize with my weaknesses, and truly understands every beat of my heart, every falter in my step, and every emotion of despair. God knows. And God reaches low to lift me back up.

Sometimes we find our comfort in pouring our hearts out in prayer. Other times we find spiritual refreshment in pouring over Scripture. And in some instances, God brings like-minded believers to us to help us on our journey to joy. Whatever means God employs to help us walk from lament and weariness to joy and resilience, it's all good. And it's all to His glory. What a Savior!

My Heart's Cry

Father, I awoke this morning with such a feeling of despair and hopelessness that I did not want to get out of bed. Help me please. I need Your grace, Your strength, Your hope, and Your joy. I never expected to experience such hopelessness, and yet here I am.

Lord, fill my heart with reminders of Your past faithfulness to me. Never let me forget the daily goodness You bless me with each morning.

I am Yours and my deepest desire is to be a light to the world and to share Your love with others. But right now, I don't believe I have anything of value to pass on to anyone. Strengthen me, revive me, and be my steady rock today and always. I know that one day I will experience a joyful heart again. Amen.

Fighting for Joy

1. *Find joy in God's past faithfulness.* Before arising from bed, purpose in your heart to spend a few moments reflecting on God's goodness to you. Intentionally recall any difficult seasons when you struggled to feel joyous about life and how God met you in that dark place and ministered to you. By faith, right now, thank Him for the good He will do through your heartache and pain.
2. *Find joy in God's present faithfulness.* Make today the day when you take small steps to know God better. Spend extended time in His Word and select several passages of Scripture that bring you comfort to meditate upon. Write these verses on cards to carry with you throughout the day and on the hour, every hour, reflect upon each promise to strengthen and encourage your faith and increase your joy.
3. *Find joy in God's future faithfulness.* Spend time reading the biblical accounts of Moses and Elijah and note how both of these godly men of faith endured seasons of great discouragement and lament. Note how they felt inadequate to the task of leading. Look at how both men desired God and followed hard after Him, even though they suffered as we do. Take special notice of the practical ways that God met their needs as physical beings, and be mindful of caring for your body, as well as your spirit, as you journey back to joy.

13

Recognize the Steadfast Love of God

Neither height nor depth, nor anything else in all creation, will be able to separate us from the love of God that is in Christ Jesus our Lord.

Romans 8:39

MY SMALL GROUP is studying a book that guides discerning believers to a better understanding of how to find peace amid difficult and unrelenting circumstances by gaining a more comprehensive understanding of God. The deeper I dive into this principle of knowing God better, I have come to believe that every committed Christian can find help, hope, and a great deal of encouragement by working through this same biblical truth.

Honestly, it's been a hard biblical concept to wrestle with. It's difficult to incorporate this into our limited human thinking and our ever-altering emotions.

The author of the book we're reading, who has endured his own share of suffering, says Scripture repeatedly supports the premise that the cure to an upset heart, including mind and emotions, is only possible with a true understanding of God. Read that again. It doesn't matter how long we suffer or from what we suffer; the well-being of our heart and soul can be tended to, healed from, and nurtured by a thorough and comprehensive knowledge of who God tells us He is in Scripture.

At first glance, some Christians might balk at such a simplistic sounding remedy to all our earthly woes. But in truth, our individual journeys to regaining consistent joy in our hearts, minds, and souls are demanding ones.

As this author noted, for believers to discover the peace that passes all understanding and joy that thrives, even in the midst of the most harrowing life circumstances, we must act. Yes, we must take steps to know our God. Remember, God's part and our part work in tandem.

As we open the Word and delve into the mysteries of God and what He says about Himself in the Old and the New Testaments, we will find an unending, yet fascinating journey before us. For those of us who have walked with the Lord for many years, we can attest to the power of the living Word of God, which reveals to our needy hearts something fresh in every reading.

Even those who read and reread the entirety of Scripture every year, find deeper divine wisdom, insight, and understanding because every word is alive, active, and powerfully God-breathed. We can count on learning something new from God's Word every day of our lives.

In this one aspect alone, God demonstrates His steadfast, persistent love for us, His beloved ones. Every single day of our lives, we must be renewed in mind and spirit by careful study of Scripture.

As we invest ourselves in this timeless spiritual discipline, we will come to more readily recognize the hand of the Lord in our everyday lives. Yes, reading, rereading, and then meditating upon God's Word will show us that "neither height nor depth, nor anything else in all creation, will be able to separate us from the love of God that is in Christ Jesus our Lord."

As we take this spiritual discipline to heart and begin to incorporate this daily habit into our lives, a fresh rhythm of hope, joy, and peace will start to emerge. We will begin to see God's everyday, steadfast love all around us. We will discover how persistent His love for us is as we drink in His new-morning mercies. We will grow more robust in our faith, more exuberant in our desire to love and serve others, and we will find our inner selves nourished and thriving once again.

Indeed, our path in fighting for joy in our everyday lives begins with knowing our God and knowing Him well. Let's begin today on a journey that will change us one verse at a time. For our God truly does love us with a steadfast, persistent love that nothing in all creation can separate us.

My Heart's Cry

Father, thank You for opening my eyes and helping me to see the steadfast and persistent love You have extended to me every day of my life. I am so grateful for Your faithful love toward me. I know that I do not deserve it. But I am thankful that You have chosen me to be part of Your forever family.

Help me, Lord, to be disciplined to search Your Scripture every day for passages that broaden and deepen my understanding of who You are. I realize that as I grow in my knowledge of You, I will find that peace that passes all understanding, I will regain the joy I have lost. I know this to be true. Please strengthen me in my daily pursuit of You. Amen.

Fighting for Joy

1. *Find joy in God's past faithfulness.* As you remember what God has done for you in the past, thank Him for His steadfast and persistent love toward you. Write your memories and your thoughts that God brings to your remembrance of specific acts of love He has bestowed upon your life. Then spend time thanking Him for who He is and who He always will be—our unchanging, faithful heavenly Father.
2. *Find joy in God's present faithfulness.* At each mealtime today, offer your thanks to God for His care for you and those you hold dear. Prayerfully ask God to open your eyes to recognize His daily goodness to you. Thank Him for His perfect provision, His perfect love, and the salvation of your soul—the gift beyond all measure. Ask Him to help you see every trial you face in light of eternity so that it does not overwhelm or render you paralyzed by discouragement or despair.
3. *Find joy in God's future faithfulness.* As you contemplate the coming months and years, do so by reminding yourself that God loves you with a steadfast, persistent, unending love. Tell yourself the truth that He will never allow anything in all creation to separate you from His love. And then give thanks to God with a joyful heart as you sit quietly in His presence and meditate on God's unchanging, magnificent character.

14

Unmovable, Unchanging

Now to him who is able to do immeasurably more than all we ask or imagine, according to his power that is at work within us, to him be glory in the church and in Christ Jesus throughout all generations, for ever and ever! Amen.

Ephesians 3:20–21

WE CAN EXPECT great things from our great God. We can and we should. Now, I'm not talking about excellent health, job promotions, perfect relationships, and hefty pay raises. No, this powerful passage of Scripture tells us that because our heavenly Father is sovereign over all and is all powerful, we can trust Him to do within us immeasurably more than we ask or imagine. What a promise!

Even though our family's lives were upended in major proportions in the last few years, I continue to find comfort and solace knowing my heavenly Father never changes. It soothes my aching soul to know, really know, that despite the ever-changing circumstances around us, I can count on God's unmovable and unchanging faithfulness toward me and my family.

Most of us would agree that change of any kind is hard. We humans are creatures of habit from the minute we wake up until when we fall asleep. If you don't believe you fall into this category, trying changing even one small habit and see how you feel.

So when God places us in a season that feels tumultuous and always shifting, like a harsh winter with no relief in sight, we can discover our Father's warm and comforting care to sustain us, despite the unpredictable conditions that surrounds us.

During those early months of unwanted change, I would wake up morning after morning reciting, "This is the day the Lord has made; I will rejoice and be glad in it" (Ps. 118:24, NKJV). As I've said before, I may have willed myself to repeat these words, hoping to actually feel "glad" but it wasn't happening. Instead, I mourned and grieved and lamented until I had no tears left to cry.

And then God began to patiently teach me something that changed me and jump-started my inner healing. Verse by verse, as I started to meditate on God's unchanging character, I slowly found myself rediscovering His goodness and tender mercies wherever I looked. Yes, even though I was in a place not of my own choosing or liking, God was molding my heart to accept His will for me. And with this molding, I slowly opened my eyes to the wonder of His unmovable and unchanging love for me.

I learned that the more time and energy I spent pouring over verses such as Ephesians 3:20, which promises us that God will do immeasurably more than we ask or imagine, that God placed His supernatural power to work within me. Body and soul, I began to regain my joy.

One of the most vital takeaways to this particular verse in Ephesians is that even though we are frail, weak, Christians, God has indeed infused His Holy Spirit power within us. As we consider this amazing and life-altering truth, we can begin to trust Him more deeply.

I would never suggest to a fellow believer that simply understanding scriptural principles makes life easier—but it does offer us a deeper measure of comfort because we can know that God will never fail us. As we persistently seek His face morning by morning, we will come to a place where His power is working so mightily inside of us that we will be changed. As we get close to our unmovable, unchanging heavenly Father, we will happily discover He is doing a work inside of us, outside of us, and all around us that truly can be described as, "immeasurably more than all we ask or imagine."

Imagine that. God has promised to do more than we can ask. More than we can imagine. All by the power He has placed within us through His Holy Spirit. This is such an important truth to latch hold of as we walk through this world of trials and sorrow.

God alone can make our hearts "glad" even when—especially when—our lives are seemingly tethered to pain and suffering. Yes, as we turn to Him, draw near to Him, and lean on Him, we can be assured that God is at work doing immeasurably more than we ask or imagine. So today, whatever burdens you are bearing, draw near to Him and let God comfort your aching heart as only He can.

My Heart's Cry

Father, there have been so many changes in our lives that I am reeling over each one. I feel overwhelmed by the loss of what was once familiar and comfortable.

Please strengthen me and help me to place the full weight of my care on Your sturdy shoulders. Help me to recognize that You are always at work doing immeasurably more than I can possibly ask or imagine.

I need Your strength every hour. And I pray that I would rediscover the joy that I have been fighting for these past months. I want to awaken every morning with a joyful, rejoicing heart that is truly glad but that will only happen as Your supernatural power works within my heart and soul. Amen.

Fighting for Joy

1. *Find joy in God's past faithfulness.* Look up the words, "unmovable" and "unchanging," and then write the definitions down. Take some time to reflect upon the meanings of these two words and how you have seen God's past work in your life demonstrate His unmovable and unchanging love toward you. Note anything you recall and write these memories in your journal.
2. *Find joy in God's present faithfulness.* Today, as you consider any difficulties and unwanted changes in your life, ask the Lord to help you reframe these challenging situations into opportunities to draw nearer to Him. Thank God for doing immeasurably more than you ask or imagine in each situation you face. Then take time to pray for great things because we serve a great God.
3. *Find joy in God's future faithfulness.* As you think about your future, note any potentially overwhelming outcomes with which you are struggling. Meditate on this verse in Ephesians and ask God to help you view these uncertainties in light of His sovereignty and power. Remind yourself that He is committed to you in an unmovable, unchanging way. God will never fail you. Then, spend time praising God for His extravagant love toward you.

15

Suffering Well

The LORD *is good to all;*
he has compassion on all he has made.

Psalm 145:9

HAVE YOU EVER considered that God is orchestrating the very suffering we are trying to run from? The full weight of answering this question assumes that first of all, we acknowledge God's sovereignty over all of life on earth and in the heavens. It also assumes the truth that God is good and what He does is good. Along with these two foundational truths, we must also seek to trust God even when we see no good from our present suffering.

As I contemplate the suffering of those dear to me, I honestly fluctuate between resting in the knowledge that God only desires good for me and those I love and the more difficult to swallow truth that God frequently uses suffering to refine us. As we try to reconcile these truths that seem to conflict, when looked at from a limited human perspective, we must develop an even deeper trust in God's glorious goodness.

I love the saints of old who shared their honest doubts, their fears, their anxieties, their weaknesses, their failures, and their burdens with us through the pages of Scripture. When we truly understand that this walk of faith through our broken and sinful world is an unending battle, we can begin to see our suffering with the eyes of enduring faith. As we turn our attention from our suffering to our suffering Savior, everything changes.

Indeed, the more swiftly we learn to avert our gaze from our sorrows to our Savior, the better we can see Jesus' redemptive plan all around us. It's true that God is absolutely sovereign over all of life on earth and in the heavens. It is just as true that God is good and what He does is good. So why is it so hard to trust Him while we are in the midst of despair and grief? That is the question for the ages, isn't it?

When we hold true to the truth found in God's Word and really believe that we can trust God to meet us exactly where we are, muddied up and disheveled though we may be, our suffering takes on a completely different tone. Think about your most recent battle with actual pain and suffering. Consider how you felt when you realized you were not in control to alleviate the pain of these heartbreaking scenarios. Helpless. Hopeless. Defeated. Despairing.

These are common human emotional responses to common human experiences. But now, factor in how completely different our suffering plays out when we walk in trust in our heavenly Father's plan for our lives. When we really believe these words, "The Lord is good to all; / he has compassion on all he has made," every aspect of our trial flips upside down.

And what is our response? Peace. Joy. Thanksgiving. Gratefulness. Humility. Surrender.

Yes, when we learn to suffer well, we will develop a deeper trust in our loving heavenly Father. We will understand and believe that God is always good and what He does is good. When we lay our faith foundation on what the Bible tells us about God's character and His perfect love for us, we will find ourselves on firm footing no matter what trials we face.

Our hearts will find their rest in Him alone, not in positive circumstances. Our hearts will discover joy that cannot be diminished. Our hearts will be joined together with Christ's, and we will begin to view our trials, troubles, and torments as temporary foes.

Yes, deeper trust is the wonderful result of learning how to suffer well. And our joy meter? Well, that will be yet another blessed benefit as we grow in grace and learn that we can trust God because He is always worthy of our trust.

It's a promise. God is good and He has compassion on all He has made. That means before, during, and after our suffering, God is good, and we will see His compassion if we have eyes to see.

My Heart's Cry

Father, help me to remember that You are in control of all things. And because of this wondrous truth, I can be at peace knowing that You only desire what is best for me. Help me to never forget that You are good and that You do good.

When I am suffering, I often lose hope and grow so weary that I just want the pain to end. Please be my strength and draw close to me in my sorrow. I need to learn to reframe every painful situation into an opportunity to trust You more deeply.

Give me the wisdom I need to view all of life through the lens of eternity, and help me to see clearly how You are always redeeming even the worst life has to offer into something beautiful in its time. Amen.

Fighting for Joy

1. *Find joy in God's past faithfulness.* Look back to when you were in the midst of a trial that was so difficult you struggled to trust the Lord. Prayerfully reflect on this painful time and ask God to help you remember how He supernaturally met you in your place of pain to comfort you. Then spend a few moments in prayer giving thanks for His compassion on you.
2. *Find joy in God's present faithfulness.* As you think about the trials that are part of your life right now, ask God to help you reframe every difficulty into something He can restore and redeem in His time. Thank Him for His goodness and love toward you. Then, by faith, thank God for answering even those prayers you haven't seen answered yet. Ask God to give you a deeper faith, a deeper trust, and the desire to suffer well.
3. *Find joy in God's future faithfulness.* Ask God to renew your joy as you look to the future knowing that God is good and He has compassion on all He has made. Ask God to refresh your outlook as you view an uncertain future, knowing that God is good and all that He does is good. Ask God to help you reframe your past seasons of suffering by teaching you to trust Him more deeply because He is always worthy of our trust.

16

Never Underestimate What God Can Accomplish

Great is our Lord and mighty in power;
his understanding has no limit.

Psalm 147:5

UNTIL RECENTLY, I never made the connection between a lack of joy and harboring bitterness and resentment. But once I did, my lack of joy made a lot more sense.

Even though it's been some years, I can still recall the betrayal I felt when I first discovered that I had been deceived repeatedly for many years by someone I called a friend. When I realized the depth of deception through some unusual circumstances, my heart shattered.

Once the revelation was in the open, I started to remember specific conversations, including some that had never made sense to me. I remember questioning the truthfulness of them at times. I tried reassuring myself that every conflict has two sides, and perhaps I simply did not have all the facts. So I let these small, frequent inconsistencies just fade to the backdrop of my life.

However, when I learned this person had lied about me, everything became very personal and hurtful. I suddenly had to reconcile the betrayal I felt by a so-called friend. I had to pray through my anger and my grief over the discovery. And then I had to work through a season when I questioned just about everyone's honesty because I felt I couldn't trust my own sense of discernment.

Over time, I thought I had moved on and had left this disagreeable exchange in the past. But I was wrong. I could tell something was off in my heart attitude because whenever this person's name was mentioned, it still stung. I was hypersensitive to anything that reminded me of how severely I had been duped.

At times, I struggled to even think about this person without feeling intensely sad or angry. Why had this happened to me? And why hadn't God protected me from this entire, distasteful situation?

I had so many questions that I took to the Lord over and over again. And yet, even when I asked God to bring healing to my hurting heart, I now know I was still clinging to "my right" to feel angry, upset, and hurt. Honestly, it is difficult for me to even admit that I was harboring bitterness and resentment against my former friend—but I was; I just didn't recognize it at the time.

And then God intervened in a way only He can do. He showed me the sinfulness of my hurting heart, and the Holy Spirit convicted me of my sin. Again, I had to go God and confess my sin of bitterness and my lingering resentment against this person. It took time for me stop "feeling" upset about this difficult situation, but finally, I did know I was free from my sin of unforgiveness.

How so? First of all, whenever I took the temperature of my emotions about this person I no longer felt hot or bothered. I realized that "There but for the grace of God, go I," and I gave thanks that in this instance I was not the perpetrator.

I finally recognized that God had allowed this painful season for my good and His glory, even if it didn't feel that way. And I realized that I now felt mercy and compassion rather than bitterness and resentment.

Looking back at the peak of my emotional pain, I felt so injured and betrayed that I believed and said these words: "I will never trust that one again. Ever."

And I meant every word. But that was then, and now it's different. Through the mighty working of our great God, I am free from the poison of bitterness and resentment. His supernatural grace has set me free. And the most telling way I know this to be true is that I have joy again.

I've learned that I underestimated what God could do in my hardened and stubborn heart. He is in the business of healing, restoring, reconciling, and rebooting entire lives through His goodness and grace. Amen to that!

So today, if you feel upset in your own heart over someone who has injured you, go to God. Don't delay. Talk to Him now, and ask Him to empower you to forgive and move on. It doesn't matter what the offense is; what does matter is that we take seriously God's mandate to forgive those who have despitefully used us.

We must forgive those who have sinned against us—for their sake and for our own. When we forgive, we are set free. When we forgive, joy will abound. When we forgive, we are most like God. Amen and amen.

My Heart's Cry

Father, only You know how many hours I have wasted mentally going over and over this offense against me. Only You understand how hurt I feel at this betrayal.

I'm reminded of David's words in the psalms, where he prays about his friend turning against him. This is perhaps the most painful aspect to this situation. It was a friend who hurt me.

Help me to move forward in complete forgiveness and give me the grace to stop dwelling on this offense. Protect me from my own sinful tendency to harbor bitterness and resentment.

Please forgive me for my hardened heart. Make it tender again and let the joy of my salvation reign supreme in my heart today and always. Amen.

Fighting for Joy

1. *Find joy in God's past faithfulness.* Remind yourself this day that God has chosen you as one of His beloved children and that you will live with Him forever throughout eternity. Thank Him that while you were still His enemy, He sent Jesus to die in payment for your sins (Rom. 5:8). Give God the thanks and glory due Him for His magnificent love toward you. Take a few moments to reflect upon how very different your life was before you became a Christian, and praise God for making you clean through the blood of Christ.
2. *Find joy in God's present faithfulness.* Today, let the Holy Spirit guide your thoughts as you reflect upon God's forgiveness toward you. Ask Him to reveal if you are holding bitterness or resentment toward anyone. Ask Him for forgiveness if you are angry over a sinful offense against you. Meditate on God's goodness in forgiving you seventy times seven and purpose to do the same toward those who may hurt you in the coming days.
3. *Find joy in God's future faithfulness.* If you are harboring emotional pain because of someone's sin against you, ask God to forgive you. Ask Him to give you a spirit of forgiveness, reconciliation, and restoration for any future conflicts with this person or others. Expect great things from our mighty God, and marvel at how your own joy will expand when you choose to forgive. Meditate on God's consistent and faithful forgiveness and offer that same forgiveness to others.

17

Where I Am Is God's Good Pleasure

God . . . is the blessed controller of all things, the king over all kings and the master of all masters.

First Timothy 6:15, PHILLIPS

DURING EVERY SEASON of life, specific challenges loom large before our eyes. When our four children were young and I was busy in the home and home schooling, I sometimes felt as though my entire life was contained within four walls.

When our children grew and left home, I felt the sting of the empty nest and its accompanying silence. When our children began having their own children, once again I knew a major life shift was transpiring—that of grandparenting.

Each of these life junctures included blessings and burdens. In those early years of 24/7 parenting, I was often sleep-deprived and functioned on autopilot. During those early empty nest years, I certainly had to wrestle through ever-changing emotions with our new status.

And today, as a grateful grandmother of seven, I am most thankful for each beloved grandchild, but I sometimes lack the energy I had as a younger woman to engage them for lengthy periods of time. Blessings and burdens—this is the stuff of life.

As I age, I've come to realize something important. Every season can be viewed through the lens of joyful thanksgiving or joyless drudgery. I remember as a young mother listening to an older, wiser, and more mature woman challenge us young moms to stop wishing for the next season to arrive. She wisely reminded us that when we were merely trying to get through the day and wishing for an easier tomorrow, we forfeited that day's joy.

It's true. When I go through my day mentally just trying to make it through, then I miss out on recognizing and relishing the goodness God constantly displays before me.

Every day, every moment, should be treasured and, more importantly, lived well. "Warts and all," as the saying goes, every day is a gift from our loving, benevolent Father. Only when we recognize this foundational truth can we see today as the beautiful opportunity God intended for us to thrive in—confines and all.

No matter how old we are, no matter what our circumstances, no matter what our station in life or what our future prospects hold, we are here today at God's good pleasure. Yes, today might be fraught with trials and temptations—or it might be filled with blessings galore. Our surroundings, our circumstances, do not change this fundamental truth: God places us exactly where He wants us to be at this moment. This truth should bring us comfort and joy.

I like this significant quotation from Andrew Murray:

> In time of trouble, say, "First, he brought me here. It is by his will I am in this strait place; in that I will rest." Next, "He will keep me here in his love, and give me grace in this trial to behave as his child." Then say, "He will make the trial a blessing, teaching me lessons he intends me to learn, and working in me the grace he means to bestow." And last, say, "In his good time he

can bring me out again. I am here (1) by God's appointment, (2) in his keeping, (3) under his training, (4) for his time."

Amen!

So for today, let us each spend time in quiet contemplation as we survey our lives at present, the blessings and the burdens alike. Let us go to God in prayer and begin thanking Him for His gracious supervision over everything, knowing He is always working for our good and His glory.

Let's not waste another moment in futile grumbling or complaints. Nor should we waste another thought on wishing today away in favor of some distant, unknown tomorrow. Rather, let us rest in the joyous truth that God is indeed the blessed Controller of all things and that He is always present with us.

My Heart's Cry

Father, please help me to discipline my heart and mind to be content in today's tasks and responsibilities. Too often I look into the future to find happiness and fulfillment when today is the only day I have been given.

Remind me that godliness with contentment is great gain. I need to stop daydreaming about an easier tomorrow when blessings abound all around me today.

Open my eyes to see Your blessed control over my days and help me to be humble and grateful for this profound truth. You alone know what is truly most beneficial to me and Your careful and very present control reveals this to me each day. Amen.

Fighting for Joy

1. *Find joy in God's past faithfulness.* Look into your past and reflect on a few of the more challenging life seasons you have experienced. Now, ask the Lord to show you how He was carefully overseeing every aspect of your life and how He cared for you despite your difficulties. Then meditate upon God's goodness as revealed through His present and perfect care for you in the past.
2. *Find joy in God's present faithfulness.* Ask the Lord to give you His perfect peace today as you survey your responsibilities for the next twenty-four hours. Ask Him to give you His grace and strength for today's tasks and for the wisdom to see His good hand of provision at every turn. Spend some quiet moments in reflection and pray for the Lord to open your eyes anew to the blessings that surround you, even amid life's burdens.
3. *Find joy in God's future faithfulness.* Find fresh hope for tomorrow by taking a deep dive into those Scripture passages that speak of God's sovereignty and love toward His beloved children. Meditate on these verses and take them with you as a reminder throughout the day that God is indeed the blessed Controller of all things and the Master above all masters. Find comfort and joy in this absolute truth because you know that God is good and all that He does is good.

18

Tender Hearts and Compassionate People

I have told you these things, so that in me you may have peace. In this world you will have trouble. But take heart! I have overcome the world.

John 16:33

WE'VE ALL HEARD the phrase, "Suffering will make you better or bitter. Your choice." Most of us have probably agreed with this summation. But this statement makes us pause if we consider it biblically. One thing to think about is where you and I land in the suffering the process. Let me explain.

When we are in the deepest throes of suffering, our thoughts and emotions and even our bodies are at their weakest and most vulnerable places. We are fighting multiple battles all at the same time.

When we hurt emotionally or physically, we are not at our prime to view our hard situation biblically. Everything becomes more difficult to process and to think about clearly. Thus, our heightened feelings, our exhausted minds, and our depleted bodies affect how we endure our suffering. This is just one facet of suffering that we must acknowledge and deal with as we endeavor to learn to suffer well.

Recently, I spoke with a young woman who is suffering severely in her first pregnancy. She is in her late thirties, and she had almost given up hope of conceiving after having been married for many years. Then God answered their prayers, and she is now expecting their first child. What should be an entirely joyous occasion has diminished into a long, drawn-out stretch of immense sickness and desperation for relief.

As we talked, I listened to this hurting and weakened mom-to-be share her hopes of getting pregnant and relishing the entire nine months of carrying a child before welcoming her little one into this world. Instead, the Lord has allowed her to suffer every day and through long sleepless nights. This young woman is not only physically ill, but she is also grieving the happy scenario of what she had imagined pregnancy would be like.

But though she is hurting, she is wise. She understands that this trial will either draw her nearer to God and into His comfort and care, or it will drag her into a pit of despair. So she fights for joy every hour.

She explained to me how even though she cannot read because she is so dizzy, she can listen to God's Word. While she cannot get outside to walk because she is so weak, she meditates on God's goodness by listening to praise music. She can't clean, do laundry, or cook, but she can keep the lines of communication open between her and her heavenly Father through prayer. This is what it looks like to fight for joy in the real world of harsh suffering and hard things.

Though my heart breaks for this woman's current suffering, I can see that God is doing something eternally beautiful within her that will affect her and all who know her. She is, by God's enabling grace, growing into the image of her Savior Jesus Christ through her suffering.

She is learning what it means to suffer well even though it's hard. And her fight for joy is winning the battle.

She will tell you that God has been doing a work within her heart that is evidenced by her newfound tenderness and compassion toward others who suffer. Once a stoic woman who rarely shared her emotions openly, she now enters in to others' pain. She is truly is growing in grace and compassion because of her present trials.

This season of hard things will pass and she knows it. However, she shared with me that many others' suffering is of the permanent and only in eternity will these other believers find absolute healing, be it emotional, mental, or physical.

Yes, my dear friend continues to suffer and it pains me to see her this way. However, she encouraged me to trust the Lord's sovereign plan for her in the midst of her pain. She showed me what it means to suffer well and to fight for joy because it matters. It makes a difference today because what we do in this life echoes throughout eternity.

My Heart's Cry

Father, my pain consumes me day and night. I feel no relief no matter what I do. I'm growing so very discouraged. I cry out to You, but still the suffering continues. Please come to my aid and help me.

I do ask You to heal me, Lord. But if You do not choose to do so, strengthen me to suffer well. Help me to keep my mind fixed on You so that I have Your peace. Give me the grace I need to keep my thoughts on You and Your promised provision and faithfulness. Show me Your kindness, Lord, by enabling me to trust You in this hard place and do a good work in my heart.

Thank You, Father, for loving me and for blessing me with joy unfailing in the midst of my pain. Amen.

Fighting for Joy

1. *Find joy in God's past faithfulness.* In your present suffering, ask God to remind you how He carefully met your every need in times past. Ask God to help you remember those specific moments when you felt hopeless to endure your trial, yet God entered in and gave you exactly what you needed. Then thank Him for His enduring and perfect love and care for you that never falters or fails.
2. *Find joy in God's present faithfulness.* Today, spend time reading the psalms and meditate upon God's glory and goodness to you. Read through several psalms and highlight the journey that the psalmist goes on as he begins with lament and then ends with shouts of joy over God's loving care toward him.
3. *Find joy in God's future faithfulness.* As you contemplate your future, be mindful about not taking on tomorrow's worries. As you fight for joy today, remember that God is in the midst of your present suffering and doing a mighty work of transformation within your heart and mind. Thank Him that He is teaching you what it means to face hard things and to suffer well as you trust Him completely.

19

Resist the Unknown Future

Though the fig tree does not bud and there are no grapes on the vines, though the olive crop fails and the fields produce no food, though there are no sheep in the pen and no cattle in the stalls, yet I will rejoice in the LORD, I will be joyful in God my Savior.

Habakkuk 3:17–18

I DO NOT believe I am alone in feeling somewhat wary of the unknowns in my future. When I survey my life and contemplate the daily struggles that are common to all, I sometimes think about my unknown tomorrows, and I rarely feel like I'll feel up to whatever comes next.

Perhaps it's my age. Or maybe what daunts me most is simply observing the pain, sorrow, and heartache that affects every person. Whatever the reason, God does not want me to be held captive by fear of tomorrow's uncertainties.

Instead, God wants me, and all of His beloved children, to find their rest, their comfort, their protection, and their joy in Him. We are not to give way to fear about our unknown futures or to even speculate as to what God may have planned for us. For when we mistakenly desire to see around the next corner, we demonstrate our lack of trust in God's faithful promise to provide for us in His way. A joyous way, to be sure.

As the passage in Habakkuk tells us, even when the trees don't bud or bear fruit, the crops fail, and no sheep or cattle are in the stalls, yet I will rejoice in the Lord, I will be joyful in God my Savior. This is one of my favorite Scripture verses because it tells me a whole lot more than simply not having enough food for today. Instead, this entire passage affirms with solidarity of purpose that I will rejoice. I will be joyful.

Countless times I have so wanted to peek around the next corner of my life, and the lives of my dear children, because I wanted to be sure we would all be okay. I realize nothing is unusual in this desire, but it does not reflect a heart that trusts in the wisdom and controlling power of our sovereign God. However, from my human perspective, it is tempting to desire to see if life events will work out as I pray they will.

Many times believers have said to me, "If only I could see the outcome of this trial, then I would be able to handle today's struggles better."

It isn't so. In fact, the opposite is more likely to be true. Even as I write these words and admit that I have wanted to peer into my future, God alone knows what it will take to mold me into the image of His dear Son. Only God truly understands and orchestrates the tiniest details of my life for what is necessary for this transformation and sanctification.

How can it be otherwise? Only our omniscient God lives in the past, present, and future. He alone allows the needed trials in my life and yours. He alone transforms these trials into the stuff that will make us more like Jesus. He alone sees all; therefore, He alone can be trusted with our unknown futures.

Right now, one of my children is suffering in ways that are unthinkable and unbearable to me as a mother. Yet I've realized as I have cried out to God to bring healing, mercy, compassion, and relief, that I have neglected to pray for my child's willingness to accept this suffering from God. I've not prayed the most courageous prayer of all, "Thy will be done."

But I've now changed my prayer focus by asking God to give my child abundant grace and strength. I've asked Him to show my dear one His glory, His goodness, and His eternal purpose through this hard season. Most of all, I have to asked God to give my child joy in Him.

Perhaps you have not yet been to a place where you have nowhere to turn except to God. But someday you will. We all get there eventually. But instead of lamenting our loss, our pain, our sorrow, we should look upwards and give thanks that God has stripped us bare of our self-sufficiency and our vain plans. Only when we are laid low will we learn that we can and must trust God for today and for our every tomorrow. Only then, will joy flourish within our hearts and minds.

My Heart's Cry

Father, when I think about the future, I feel so unsettled. Especially when life today seems so hard, and I often don't have the strength I need to face these challenges.

I don't want to feel afraid of what might or might not happen. Help me to find my peace, my joy, my everything in You alone. Guide my thoughts this day and enable me to keep my eyes on You only. When I start to feel my emotions unraveling, remind me, dear Father, of Your great love for me. Strengthen me to desire Your will above my own, always. Amen.

Fighting for Joy

1. *Find joy in God's past faithfulness.* As you consider your life today, think to those past seasons when you didn't know what your life would look like. Remember how you felt, the uncertainty you battled, the fear you experienced. Then recall how God met you in that place of vulnerability and how He walked with you through each step of uncertainty to a place of firm footing close beside Him.
2. *Find joy in God's present faithfulness.* Take some time today to contemplate your current challenges, no matter what form they may take. Ask the Lord to help you lay each burden down at His feet and for the wisdom and grace to leave them there. Pray for the understanding and wisdom you need to walk sure-footed in faith as you trust God day by day.
3. *Find joy in God's future faithfulness.* As you think about your future unknowns, thank the Lord for His promises to provide for your every need. Take some time to search out Scripture that reinforces this biblical truth. Write these passages out and place them around your home, in your car, or wherever you spend the most time. Read and reread them. Meditate upon their powerful truths. Then thank God for His promise to never, ever leave or forsake you.

20

Be Present, Be All There—*Today*

This is the day the L*ORD has made.*
We will rejoice and be glad in it.

Psalm 118:24, NKJV

SOMETIMES WE must take practical steps in our journey to fight for joy. We can invest our time and energy in studying God's Word, praying, praise and worship, meditating, and journaling. These are the fundamental spiritual disciplines that we should develop into our daily lives, no matter how long we have walked with the Lord.

Each of these components keeps us in check with the Spirit. Each of these parts provides more opportunity for us to grow and know God more accurately and intimately. Each of these should be a priority from the moment we open our eyes until we lie down to rest at night. Yes, as we fight for joy, every one of these elements of the Christian walk is essential.

However, we need to take other steps to grow in our joy as well. Before we address some of these, let's go back to the garden of Eden and revisit the impact that gaining knowledge had on Adam and Eve and eventually, the entire human race.

Before Adam and Eve disobeyed God's directive to not eat of the knowledge of good and evil, they were completely innocent. They did not understand the weight they would carry for their entire lives once their eyes were opened to the knowledge of good and evil.

When they disobeyed God and gave in to Satan's lies and temptations, everything changed. They now knew they had sinned. They now knew they were guilty. They now had the knowledge of good and evil, and they were ashamed.

We all understand the full weight their disobedience had on the human race. But let's focus on the weight that gaining knowledge of good and evil had on them, and eventually, us.

From that moment, Adam and Eve were no longer sinless, perfect beings. Rather, their sin stained them in every way conceivable, and it destroyed the peace that God had intended for them and His created world. They disobeyed and were punished for their actions. Part of their punishment may very well be the simple understanding of good and evil.

Today we face a similar "knowledge" as we are daily, hourly, and minute-by-minute bombarded with information too weighty, too burdensome, and often too horrendous for us to shoulder. If you haven't yet guessed where this is heading, it's a warning to all of us to use technology wisely.

When we choose to mentally engage in worldwide disasters, political or otherwise, it affects our joy. When we opt to have an online presence day and night, it affects our joy. When we place a higher priority on browsing the Internet than seeking the Lord and His presence, it affects our joy.

Today's instant knowledge availability is indeed its own particular form of punishment, and it's mostly self-inflicted. Not only is the online world a dark voice that frequently silences the beauty of today, it is also a distracting one.

If we desire to walk in joy, then we must make some difficult choices. Our heart must first choose God, His Word, prayer, praise and worship, meditating, and even journaling over the 24/7 invasive information explosion available at our fingertips.

If we want to say with the psalmist, "This *is* the day the LORD has made. / We will rejoice and be glad in it," then we have to re-evaluate how many of our hours we waste on gaining knowledge that only distracts and discourages us from the goodness God has bestowed upon our lives.

Yes, too much knowledge of world, national, state, city, and local events is simply too much. None of us was created to bear the burdens of such difficult and incrementally weighty knowledge of evil. God alone can bear the world's burdens. And we are not God.

So beginning today, take some time to sit in silence and prayerfully ask God to reveal to you the changes you need to make in your intake of news. Ask Him to show you how detrimental it is in your fight for joy. Then courageously start to adjust how much knowledge and information you ingest every day. Your journey to joy depends upon it.

My Heart's Cry

Father, I know that I spend far too much time listening to newscasts and reading about world events on my phone. I want to know what is happening around the world, but I realize the more knowledge I have, the more burdened I become.

I feel the pain of those suffering throughout the world and I do pray for these dear people. But I also realize that I cannot handle this much negative news every day.

Help me to discipline myself to stay away from too much online activity and to increase the time I spend reading Your Word and praying. Make me sensitive and alert to Your Holy Spirit's warnings to turn away from sinful reports and images that will only deplete my joy.

Instead, help me to be present today and to rejoice in this day because You have made it. Amen.

Fighting for Joy

1. *Find joy in God's past faithfulness.* Spend a few moments giving thanks to God for this day and the possibilities it brings. Ask the Lord to open your eyes to ways He has been close to you when you needed Him most. Pray that God will give you the grace to rejoice in this day and not get distracted by the world's suffering and the world's woes. Focus only on God and His glory and grandeur.
2. *Find joy in God's present faithfulness.* Today, be intentional about being fully present in your life wherever God has placed you. Rather than nurturing a discontented or disgruntled spirit because of the hardships you face, ask God to fill your heart and mind with a spirit of thanksgiving. Then, praise God for the gift of another day. Ask Him to fill you with the joy of His Spirit and ask Him for eyes to see Him at work all around you.
3. *Find joy in God's future faithfulness.* Sometime this week, get away from the noise of the world—whether it be other people, the news, or your phone—and ask God to quiet your heart, mind, and soul. Pray about everything and anything you worry or feel burdened about and confess your lack of faith. Meditate upon the command, "Be still and know that I am God" (Ps. 46:10). No matter how frightening the world may become, remind yourself that God is on the throne and ruling over every atom of creation. Then repeat the verse, "The joy of the Lord is my strength" (Neh. 8:10), with the knowledge that this joy does not depend upon favorable circumstances.

21

Understand God's Perfect Provision

And God will wipe away every tear from their eyes; there shall be no more death, nor sorrow, nor crying. There shall be no more pain, for the former things have passed away.

Revelation 21:4, NKJV

IT'S BEEN OVER twenty years ago and I can still remember the term I coined for my beloved father-in-law's death. He suffered a "good death."

What exactly did I mean by this phrase? Well, anyone who was close to my father-in-law knew him as a kind, quiet man. He was also a man given to lengthy spells of depression that debilitated him. I had known him for twenty-five years when he passed away. And truthfully, most of the years he was simply incapacitated by his just-under-the-surface depression or deeply mired in the strongholds of it.

But God. Isn't this always the case? About eight years before he died, Jesus saved my father-in-law after he heard the gospel message yet again at the church he attended with his second wife.

From that moment, my father-in-law was a dynamically changed man. The Spirit did a transformative work in his life and everyone witnessed it.

We thanked God often for rescuing him from the clutches of sin and saving him forevermore. We got to be up close and personal with him as we observed the Holy Spirit's sanctifying power in his life. Jesus Christ changed everything about this beloved man.

While we were at a funeral, grieving the loss of my husband's grandfather, my dear father-in-law broke the news that he was dying of esophageal cancer and only had months to live. It was such a striking and bittersweet revelation because my father-in-law was in perfect peace about his terminal diagnosis.

During those last five months of his life, I spent quite a bit of time with him, running him to appointments and cancer treatments—and I marveled. He was no longer a man given to severe valleys in his emotions. Nor was he a man who was angry at God or depressed about his life being cut short so suddenly.

Rather, my kindly father-in-law was at peace and was joyful. We enjoyed many conversations about the wonder of Christ and of eternity. We talked and talked about Jesus being all we need. We conversed about faith and family in such a way that at times, I felt almost envious that he would see Jesus before me.

Right until he died, he exhibited the God-given grace to suffer and die well because he was certain he knew where he was going. He died a good death, and his example continues to impact me today.

When we know someone we love dearly is facing death, it will go one of two ways. If our loved one is one of God's own beloved children, forgiven through Christ's perfect sacrifice, then this individual will have peace. He or she will experience joy.

If, on the other hand, our dear one doesn't have a saving faith in Jesus Christ and has not repented and believed, then peace has no part in the person's journey to death. So, today, when the opportunity arises, and I can speak of the saving work of Christ on the cross, I do.

And in those moments when someone I love dearly has been drawn by the Holy Spirit to repent and believe, I rejoice. I always think of my father-in-law and the supernatural grace and strength and joy that God blessed him with those final months of his life on earth.

Some days, my own fight for joy wavers and then I think of him, and I smile. I, too, anticipate the moment when I enter eternity and my tears will be wiped dry, sorrow will cease, and pain will be no more—for the former things have passed away. What joy!

My Heart's Cry

Father, my heart is near to breaking when I consider the pain my beloved one is enduring. Please draw near to this one and ease his or her suffering. Comfort this one. Comfort us.

Help us one and all to keep our eyes firmly on Jesus both day and night. Give us Your grace and strength to see Your perfect hand of provision, even in this time of suffering and grief.

Enable us to see with eyes of faith and to speak boldly about Your saving grace. Stay near to us during our sorrow and fill us with Your abundant joy.

Continue to do a good work within all our hearts as we walk our loved one to eternity. Please, Lord, come close. Amen.

Fighting for Joy

1. *Find joy in God's past faithfulness.* Reflect on the past, when the events in your life felt so sorrowful and filled with grief that you didn't have the strength to move forward. Then, ask God to show you how He entered the situation as only He can do and lifted you with His grace and goodness. Prayerfully ask the Lord to bring to your remembrance even the smallest new-morning mercies He compassionately bestowed on you and your loved ones. Then, spend time in praise and worship for His perfect provision and the joy you experienced.
2. *Find joy in God's present faithfulness.* Today, ask the Lord to lighten your burdens. Ask Him to show you how to cast every care into the faithful arms of Christ and leave it there. When sorrow and grief threaten to overwhelm, run to the psalms and read these powerful accounts of transformation from abject grief to joyful exclamation. Then, thank God for the good work He is doing in your life and in your loved ones' lives. Remember to count it all joy as we journey through heartbreak and grief because you know where you will be in eternity.
3. *Find joy in God's future faithfulness.* When life seems to be so painful, purposefully remember that God is the one who saves, forgives, restores, and rescues for all eternity. Lean hard into the Bible passages that tell of God's sovereignty and mighty power. Meditate upon Scripture verses that share the hope of heaven and the eternal security every believer has in Jesus Christ. Then spend time giving thanks to the One who promises to overcome the world's troubles and blesses us with joy unstoppable.

22

Joy that Doesn't Depend on Circumstances

No one will take your joy from you.

John 16:22, ESV

AFTER I HAD BEEN sick with the flu for over a week and still felt weak from the virus, my husband left for church without me. As I recuperated (and lamented about how hard this bug had hit me), I started to wallow in self-pity. *Oh Lord, please heal me. Oh Lord, please strengthen me. Oh Lord, this is just awful, help me. Oh Lord, haven't I suffered enough?*

I'm not ashamed that I'm sensible enough to cry out to my Lord and Savior when in distress. However, after my husband arrived home from church that morning, I was rightly ashamed. Lying down with a splitting headache and the residual effects of this hard-hitting virus, I asked my husband about his time at our church. He got choked up as he related the following conversation to me.

One of our fellow church families is undergoing numerous trials that are each life-threatening and life-changing. My husband shared how this family is facing a parent's cancer diagnosis, a child with cancer, a job loss, and other heart-wrenching costly setbacks. And yet, the father fairly glowed with the joy of the Lord. My husband couldn't contain his amazement as he recounted this to me.

I asked questions and thoughts about the trials this family is facing continued to mount in my heart and head. I then prayed for them, and as I did, my own heart was rightly convicted. I realized that I often have made pursuing good health as an idol of my heart.

Yes, it's right to take good care of our bodies for they are the temple of the Holy Spirit. And yes, it's good to do our utmost to stay healthy and strong so that we can serve the Lord with our best efforts, time, and talents. However, whenever we make anything so important that we lose our joy when our "idol" lets us down, that's sin.

So I had to reckon with my sadly lacking heart attitude that had just earlier that morning complained to God about how sick I was. Instead choosing to worship God, I chose to whine. Shame on me.

The remainder of that day I contemplated how often I allow my hard circumstances to steal my joy when things are not of my liking or my choosing. And let's be honest, how often for any of us does life hand us favorable circumstances for any lengthy space of time. It's rare. For life here on planet earth is hard and has been so since the beginning.

We believers, though, are given the supernatural joy that doesn't depend upon favorable circumstances, and this truth changes everything. As this short verse in John states, "No one will take your joy from you." No one. Nothing. Not ever.

It's hard to fathom that those around us who are facing life-threatening and life-changing circumstances can emit such resilient joy that even fellow believers are in awe of it. But it's true. It's available. It's a promise from our heavenly Father, and when our joy is found in God alone, no one or nothing can disturb it.

I mulled over this principle for quite a while and found myself confessing my lack of faith, my discontent, and my lack of joy to God. I then asked Him to infuse me with His supernatural joy that never, ever, depends upon circumstances.

I spent time praying for this family who is facing so much more than I am, and above all, I asked the Lord to do such a miraculous work in their hearts that no one or nothing could steal their joy in the coming weeks and months. *Oh Lord, don't allow anyone or anything to steal their joy.*

May God help us all to so fix our gaze on Jesus that come what may, we too, are filled with joy inexpressible and so full of glory that it cannot be contained. Amen.

My Heart's Cry

Father, please forgive me for focusing on my trials instead of keeping my gaze fixed on Jesus. Help me, Lord, to choose better in the coming days. Give me Your divine wisdom to know that everything You allow to touch me even when it hurts is for my ultimate good.

Grow my faith through these difficult times and enable me to face my hardships with resilience and hope and fullness of joy. Show me Your glory, Lord! Reveal Your Father's heart to me when I am feeling overwhelmed and afraid. Walk closely by my side and hold me close always. Amen.

Fighting for Joy

1. *Find joy in God's past faithfulness.* Recount God's past faithfulness toward you by taking time to think of earlier days when you were in the midst of trials with no apparent way out. Write down how God met you in your vulnerability and met your every need. Then spend time in praise and worship over the grandeur and glory of God and how His love never fails.
2. *Find joy in God's present faithfulness.* Give yourself time to be alone with the Lord today so that you can quiet your heart and mind and avert your focus from your problems to the Problem Solver. With your Bible open, spend time in quiet reflection as you read through the book of Psalms and note how each psalm is a story with lament and then victory. Place your focus on Jesus alone. Then thank Him for His constant, unwavering intercession for all that concerns you.
3. *Find joy in God's future faithfulness.* Prayerfully give thanks for the God's future provision even though you can't see it, touch it, or even imagine it. Tell Him of your love and worship for His unchanging character. Ask Him to continue to sanctify you as you continue to walk with Him day by day. Pray for a robust faith and an unwavering, resilient joy that is never dependent upon circumstances.

23

Release Control and Outcomes

Trust in the Lord *and do good; Dwell in the land and feed on His faithfulness. Delight yourself also in the* Lord*, and He shall give you the desires of your heart.*

Psalm 37:3–4, NKJV

OVER THE PAST fifteen years women have come and gone from my midweek study. Life seasons change and responsibilities ebb and flow, as do the women who enter our Bible and book study group. But as I reflect upon these diverse women from different walks of life and at unique stages of their Christian walk, one common challenge rises above all others: We women have to fight against the desire to be in control.

As far back as the garden of Eden, when God rendered judgment on Adam and Eve, God told Eve that from that moment forward women would want to usurp control over their spouses. Now this is just one area of life that women struggle to control. Consider that this very desire for control is at work everywhere in our lives—because it is.

To be fair, women are deeply relational and thus, highly invested in their families, friends, and others. So it makes perfect sense to want to jump in and fix what requires repair and manage what seems out of control. And there's the rub.

Of the numerous women with whom I've had the privilege to study God's Word, it never takes long before we circle back around to the topic of letting go of control (or our misconception of being in control). We all realize it. We all fight against it, for when we seek for control we say two important things: First, we are, by omission, admitting that we do not trust God and His plan for our lives. Second, we are also saying that we are wiser than God and know better how to solve our problems and those of whom we love.

Neither of these false beliefs help us in our fight for joy. Rather, they contribute to stifling joy from the very core of our beings. The more we labor with human strength to control outcomes and make things all better, in the same measure, we inadvertently derail the good and worthy work God desires to do within our hearts and lives.

So what's the path to peace and joy everlasting? It's simple. "Trust in the LORD and do good; / Dwell in the land and feed on his faithfulness." As we read this brief passage from the Psalms, we discover a bountiful lesson in living free of the burden of control and free of the burden of ensuring preferred outcomes.

I like the old saying that reminds us, "God is the blessed controller of all things." We all need this reminder each day. When I put my full trust in God's plan for me today, the easier my soul and spirit rest, despite the hardships I face. The more I resist God's plan for me today, the harder my soul and spirit wrestle and lose in the futile and frustrating attempt.

Perhaps the most comforting phrase in this particular psalm are these words, "feed on his faithfulness." As we begin trusting in the Lord rather than our plans to take control, we can then turn our attention to others' needs and do good to them. We dwell in the land where God has placed us, and we then can feed on His faithfulness.

What exactly does this mean?

We learn to breathe in His goodness and exhale the same. We choose to trust God with our needs and start serving others with our benefits and blessings. And then, we feed on the faithfulness of God's good Word, His promises eternal, and rediscover that our joy will flourish within these simple yet powerful safeguards.

Indeed, women will always need to be on the alert against usurping control and seeking to run over others' plans and preferences in favor of their own. The more we head off this sinful tendency to try to take control, God will bless our obedience by bestowing on us joy eternal. Joy everlasting. Joy overflowing. Joy in abundance and joy that cannot be dimmed or diminished by life's circumstances. And let's be honest. Isn't that what we all desire?

My Heart's Cry

Father, today I am working hard to not involve myself in matters too great for me. I know that You want me to trust You with everything large and small in my life. Why is it so difficult to keep my hands off difficult situations?

I am trying to lay my burdens down and wait in faith while You do the work that needs to be accomplished. It feels all wrong to sit and be still, but I know You want me to rest in Your absolute power and control.

Give me Your wisdom. Give me Your grace. Help me to submit myself to You in every situation, and as I do, I know my joy will flourish and grow. Only when I place myself under Your rightful authority and trust You fully can I ever know perfect peace and joy forevermore. Amen.

Fighting for Joy

1. *Find joy in God's past faithfulness.* Take time this morning to reflect deeply upon the goodness and glory of God. Do a word search and locate as many verses on these two character qualities of God. Read verse by verse aloud. Then take some time to reflect upon the magnitude of God's glory and grandeur and how from the very beginning of time God has demonstrated His perfect love toward mankind.
2. *Find joy in God's present faithfulness.* Write down each challenge you face today. Then, pulling from the verses you found on God's goodness and glory, select passages that bring joy and peace to you. Meditate on each verse you have paired with your challenges. Then pray through your doubts, fear, and worries. Both figuratively and literally, hand these problems to God, and then turn your attention to dwelling in the land, serving others, and feeding on His faithfulness.
3. *Find joy in God's future faithfulness.* Rather than peering into the unknown and uncertain future, and thus fueling doubts, fear, and worry, choose to feast upon the eternal promises found throughout God's Word. Take time to meditate, memorize, and carry with you those particular promises that comfort you. Then begin a time of praise and thanksgiving to God by reciting and recounting His past acts of love, generosity, and faithfulness toward you. Feed on these remembrances and watch how your joy overflows.

24

God as Our Defender

In you, O Lord, do I take refuge; let me never be put to shame; in your righteousness deliver me! Incline your ear to me; rescue me speedily! Be a rock of refuge for me, a strong fortress to save me!

Psalm 31:1–2, ESV

ONE OF THE most difficult lessons my friends and family and I have learned over the past few years has been to allow God to be our defender. Certainly, everyone has been hurt by others' unkind words and deeds. Of course, living in a fallen world, we experience the painful repercussions of others' sinful words, attitudes, and actions. None of us remains unscathed our entire lives.

However, when we humbly and obediently follow the Bible's directives on how life within a church body should be modeled, and then we face rejection or worse from fellow Christians, it's heartbreaking. None of us ever expects to be lied about and maligned by fellow believers. But it happens often in the church.

My husband and I have been so blessed by our long friendships with those who serve in full-time ministry positions. Several of our friends are pastors of churches, others are missionaries, and others work with youth and college students. These faithful men and women who have taken the call to give their lives away every day to the Lord and His service. They are beautiful souls.

We have shared countless conversations, meals, service opportunities, and have gratefully worshiped together through the years. We know these individuals intimately. While they are diverse in personality, giftedness, and in nearly every other human way, they have in common their passion for serving Christ wherever that may take them. They are my heroes on so many levels.

And yet, for all their differences, they have one life experience in common. Each has been at the receiving end of slander, gossip, and ungodly treatment—by their churches, sending missionary organizations, and those who commission them to go and make disciples. This should not be.

Truly, we have been privy to similar unbiblical and rebellious situations secondhand through our many friends who have been on the receiving end of the sinfulness by disobedient believers. But when it came home to us, it broke my heart and stole my joy. Throughout the past two years, God has been pruning my heart and He hasn't stopped yet. He has been revealing to me not others' sins and failings but my own.

I have felt as though I have been under the Potter's hand being molded, stripped bare, and remade again and again. And I know it is for my own good and God's glory. I have learned an important lesson these past months. God has shown me that I care too much about others' opinion of me.

I have been tempted many times to prove my innocence and make sure that everyone knew we did what was right according to biblical mandates. This passion to defend myself took my joy, and I've had to fight to regain it—but not without cost.

Ever so slowly, God has worked within my troubled heart and set me free from this compulsion to defend myself. He has done something within my hurting heart that no amount of explaining and convincing could ever accomplish. I've learned that God is my defender. He alone knows the truth. He can and will carry my pain and bring healing in His own time and manner. And that's all I need. It's all you need as well.

As we walk through this valley of sorrow and tears, I pray we never underestimate the good that God can accomplish through our most difficult trials. I pray we never forget the wonder of the God we serve. He decides what will be allowed and what we will be spared from in this life. We must, for the sake of our fight for joy, learn to place the full weight of our trust, our faith, and our very hope in Him alone. And as Scripture tells us, God will never disappoint us.

My Heart's Cry

Father, help me to put the full weight of my trust in You alone. Help me to trust You with this hard and painful situation I find myself in. I cannot sleep at night for worrying about what others are thinking and saying about me.

Please, Lord, protect and shelter me. Defend me. You know the truth. You can carry this pain and bring healing from it. Help me to lay down my desires to be proven right and to be found innocent. I am weary of thinking of this problem and the repercussions it brings. I pray that I can lay it down at Your feet and leave it there. Thank You, Lord, for Your constancy and care for me. My hope is in You. Amen.

Fighting for Joy

1. *Find joy in God's past faithfulness.* As you consider past seasons of suffering and sorrow, ask God to bring to your mind specific provisions from Him that made all the difference. Ask Him to remind you of how He tenderly loved you and showered you with care and compassion especially tailored to your specific needs. Then spend time thanking Him for His gracious fatherly care for you.
2. *Find joy in God's present faithfulness.* Take time to sit in silence before the Lord and ask Him to reveal to you anything that troubles you. Large and small, bring each matter before Him. Tell Him how you feel. Tell Him what you're afraid of. Tell Him your heart. Then tell Him what you most appreciate about Him. Thank Him for His goodness, His grace, His power, His provision, His love, and His forgiveness.
3. *Find joy in God's future faithfulness.* As you consider the future, invest in protecting and promoting a joyous attitude by creating a journal of joy verses. Spend time researching specific portions of Scripture that bring you joy and copy them into a journal. Find a new verse every day for a month. Once your journal of joy is complete, read it every day and meditate on one verse to keep your heart and mind on God's perfect protection and provision for you.

25

Trade Losses for Lessons

I appeal to you therefore, brothers, by the mercies of God, to present your bodies as a living sacrifice, holy and acceptable to God, which is your spiritual worship.

Romans 12:1, ESV

HAVE YOU considered that our desire for comfort often overrides our desire for sanctification? Think about this; what is the first and primary desire of our hearts during a time of real testing and suffering? Relief, right? Fast, swift, and sure relief. I doubt any of us could deny that our default response to any form of pain and suffering is to find relief, escape, or an end to the pain we find ourselves mired in.

I'd never given this penchant for longing for release from suffering much thought until I read a quotation by Randy Alcorn saying that Christians frequently place a much higher value on seeking relief from our suffering than we do on obtaining personal holiness.

He is right. When we rightly value the sanctifying process of Holy Spirit in our lives, we can view our trials differently. They may not cease and desist, but we can view them through a heavenly perspective.

Instead of seeking every avenue under the sun to find escape from our pain, we can look toward the heavens and pray that God will strengthen us to endure our trial and thus emerge stronger. If our goal is to be transformed into the image of Jesus Christ, then suffering will be our daily companion throughout our lives. If we, however, choose to seek instant relief rather than submitting to the Lord's plan for us, we won't learn the lessons God intends for us to glean.

Truly, this is a foundational biblical principle. Throughout the Bible, we can read how God forged His great men and women of faith through the suffering they endured. They, like us, probably didn't want to suffer. They, like us, probably wanted to short-circuit their seasons of suffering in exchange for a trouble-free existence. But that is not God's plan for His people.

As we read here in Romans 12:1, our act of spiritual worship means we must willingly surrender our rights to our very lives and submit to God's perfect plan for each of us. We must willingly (joyfully even) present ourselves as a living sacrifice to God each day. As we learn to position ourselves under the mighty hand of God every day, He then transforms our losses into lessons that will transform us.

Often, I believe we pursue the path of least resistance by attempting to take control of and limit our suffering by any means possible. But I wonder if that would change if we began to place a higher value on holiness. If we truly believe God only desires the best for us, then we can reframe our seasons of suffering to reflect a submissive, trusting, and joyful heart.

Only as we study these biblical principles daily, can we hope to be renewed in our thinking and transformed from the inside out. Only then can we discover that our joy is not contingent on gaining relief or escape from that which pains us.

I pray that each of us learns this important truth and we begin to view our hardships through the lens of eternity. For the Bible tells us God is indeed preparing us for the next life, our heavenly eternal life. Oh, what a Savior! Oh, what a mighty God we serve. May we cling to Him in our pain and suffering and confidently trust that He will make all things beautiful in His time.

My Heart's Cry

Father, today I am facing such overwhelming circumstances that I know I do not have the strength or the energy to endure them. Please draw near to me now and lend me Your grace and Your strength. Help me to run to Your arms when I feel undone and overcome by suffering and pain.

Give me Your wisdom and understanding so that I do not sin in my heart against You. Show me how to endure these hard things and to trust You to teach me lessons I cannot learn any other way. Be my strength, my hope, my help. And give me what I need to suffer well, so I can grow in holiness. Support me, Lord, with Your constancy and care. Amen.

Fighting for Joy

1. *Find joy in God's past faithfulness.* Ask God to reveal to you how He worked in your heart and mind through past seasons of suffering. Pray that God would show you how He was working in and through your suffering to teach you important lessons. Then recall how your losses were transformed by God's supernatural work of sanctification. Ask yourself how you have used what you have learned to encourage and comfort others.

2. *Find joy in God's present faithfulness.* Today ask the Lord to give you the courage to pray, "Thy will be done," rather than being focused solely on seeking relief from your suffering. Ask the Lord to give you the divine wisdom you require to see, really see, how God is using these difficulties to transform you into the image of Jesus. Then, by faith, thank Him in advance for the good work He is accomplishing within you for your good and His glory.
3. *Find joy in God's future faithfulness.* As you consider your unknown future, pray that God will grant you a spirit of quiet confidence and peace. Ask Him to bring to your remembrance all the good He has accomplished during your seasons of suffering. Then thank Him for the ongoing work of sanctification He is doing in your heart and mind today. Praise God for the losses you have endured and the lessons that have brought you joy unshakable. Purpose to view any future hardships with a thankful heart that fully trusts in the goodness of our heavenly Father.

26

Know the Times and Seasons

Yet he did not leave himself without witness, for he did good by giving you rains from heaven and fruitful seasons, satisfying your hearts with food and gladness.

Acts 14:17, ESV

AFTER ENDURING a season of suffering (or watching those you love suffer), we can easily fall into the lie that whatever we face today will last forever. But it won't. Suffering has an end date. It does.

Although understanding this to be true doesn't take away the sting of today's pain, does it? Randy Alcorn wrote in his book, *90 Days of God's Goodness,* that Christians frequently stop time in their minds when they face hardship and suffering.

I agree. We tend to adopt this mindset by default without giving it much critical thought. But it's a joy-killer.

As we think about the suffering in our lives and in those we care about, the suffering meter can appear to be over the chart—unending, incalculable, unimaginable, overwhelming. And it can feel that way for days, weeks, and months on end. Again, when we focus on our pain (instead of on who God is), it's a joy killer.

We lose hope. We lose spiritual ground. We lose our perspective and our resiliency to fight for joy.

So how do we maintain our spiritual equilibrium amid all the suffering and sorrow that blankets our lives? We look for God's good testimony amid the hardships. We choose to focus on God's goodness. We become faithful rememberers who can recall and recite God's faithfulness in ways both small and large.

When we look around and all we see is suffering, we are not looking closely enough. It's so easy to see the disastrous and the desperate around us. But we have to hone our spiritual eyes to see, really see, what God is doing (what He promises to do) so that we do not fall into despair.

A while back I was struggling with personal suffering and trials that felt all the harder because of my friends' suffering. I got up in the morning and immediately recounted the prayers for myself and my dear ones from the night before. I lie in bed interceding for help, for rescue, for relief. Literally, I would beg Him to intervene.

Sometimes God did answer my prayers for rescue and relief. At other times the suffering continued. In a few cases, the suffering grew more intense. Through each of these hard situations though, I learned to see, really see, God's good handiwork. I learned to remember better as I started reflecting and recounting His past goodness to me and them.

The more diligently I looked for God's goodness in the everyday and the mundane, the more my joy filled my heart with love, hope, and peace. I experienced a fresh settledness deep within my heart because I knew this season was just that—a season.

As we study the Old and New Testaments, we can read about biblical characters and discover how their lives were riddled with sorrow. These men and women faced hardships we face today.

In particular, as we delve deeply into the book of Psalms, we can see how the writers experienced the highs and lows of daily life. These men endured the gamut of emotions. They hurt as we do. They were confused as we often are. They also felt like their suffering would never end—as we mistakenly do. And yet, as we read their stories, we discover the wonder and beauty of God's intervention, His rescue and the relief He brought them in His time.

Like us, their joy waxed and waned, according to what was happened in their lives. And also like us, they had to discipline themselves to keep their eyes on God, their focus on His faithfulness, and their joy in Him.

So today, when we are tempted to believe the lie that our present season of suffering is forever, let us cast off that untruth and cling to Jesus. Let us each draw near to God through prayer and supplication and stay close to Him. Let us ask God to give us eyes to see all He has done, all He is doing, and all He has promised to do.

My Heart's Cry

Father, I feel so discouraged by the suffering I am mired in today. I feel like it will last forever. I can do nothing to stop what is happening to me and all around me. I am truly at Your mercy.

Please, Lord, help me to draw close to You during this time of hardship. Help me to see, really see, all the goodness You have bestowed upon my life. Open my eyes to see Your glory, Lord. Show me how to walk through this valley in a way that brings You glory and restores my joy. My days and hours are in Your hands, and I am thankful for that truth. Please strengthen my heart and give me what I need to walk in such a way that I always give You the thanksgiving and glory You are owed. Amen.

Fighting for Joy

1. *Find joy in God's past faithfulness.* Become a good rememberer as God told the Israelites to be. Seek to accurately remember and then contemplate God's goodness and grace toward you and those you love. Document these pivotal moments from your past when you really saw God's faithfulness revealed to you.
2. *Find joy in God's present faithfulness.* Show yourself to be a faithful rememberer of God's past goodness to you by accepting today's suffering as part of His perfect plan for you at this time. Resist the temptation to seek rescue from your hardships. Pray that God will give you eyes to see that today's hardships are not permanent. Remind yourself of the biblical stories of faithful men and women and how they traversed through their own seasons of suffering only to emerge stronger in their faith.
3. *Find joy in God's future faithfulness.* Purpose to be joyful in the coming days. Seek the Lord both day and night and pour out your heart to Him. Tell Him of your worries, fears, and concerns. Ask Him to fill you with His supernatural power and strength to face future suffering with a heart fully confident in Him alone. Then thank God for choosing you to be one of His beloved children whom He has promised to love and care for throughout all eternity. What a joy to contemplate!

27

See the Good, Even in the Hard

Be strong and courageous . . . for the Lord your God goes with you; he will never leave you nor forsake you.

Deuteronomy 31:6

HEARTBREAKING EVENTS HAVE occurred more times than I can count in our lives, regarding my husband's job. My husband has been a high school mathematics teacher for forty years, and through the years has come home with the devastating news that a student committed suicide.

Each time, we grieve for the respective families' loss and then we pray. For years, I would say I cannot imagine a more heart-rending message to receive than finding out your child has taken his or her own life.

Some years later, we found out the abject pain of such a loss when three of our extended family members took their lives. I don't think our family will ever be the same again. I know the immediate family members are changed forever; how can they not be?

And yet, I have witnessed how even in the midst of such grief God shows up. Because that's who He is. Our God is our personal heavenly Father who promises to never, ever leave or forsake us. As I contemplate the healing process that has occurred over the years since these suicides, one truth shines brightly above all others. God sees. God cares. Only God can heal.

I have realized that even in the midst of the unthinkable pain and suffering this life brings, nothing is a match for the supernatural grace, goodness, and faithfulness of God. He alone can restore lost hope, lost faith, lost joy. And He does so with great power and might.

Since each of us has our own unique path of trials to traverse, it's good to know that God will never leave or forsake us even when we can barely put one foot in front of the other.

I love this passage from Deuteronomy 31:6. It's both a remarkable and a beautifully stated truth. Why? Because Scripture tells us that God is with us. God is never distant or distracted. He is never focused on worldwide events instead of seeing our struggles. Through careful study of God's Word we see about His love, forgiveness, faithfulness, compassion, and tender care for us.

Truth be told, we can do hard things even in the hardest of times because God gives us the ability to see the good even in the hard. He alone can open our eyes to see and find renewed hope and joy in His perfect plan and His perfect provision. What a Savior! What a God we serve!

So today, if you feel discouraged, depressed, and overwhelmed by this season of suffering and grief, take heart. Bow your heart and mind to the God of heaven and earth and ask Him to send you reminders of His great and gracious love for you.

While there is no limit on grief it can be tempered by the goodness God blesses you and me with every day. Remember the verse from Lamentations about new-morning mercies? It's true. Every day, God has prepared in advance new-morning mercies for us to find renewal and refreshment in our spirits.

As we look for the good even in the hard, we will discover a fresh intimacy and closeness with our beloved heavenly Father. Our joy will abound as we set our face upon Jesus, knowing that even right now, this very minute, Jesus lives to intercede for us. Yes, even in our most heartbreaking life experiences, we can see the good even in the hard. Why? Because God is with us.

My Heart's Cry

Father, we are struggling such pain in this season of loss. Our family is hurting beyond what I have ever imagined. Please draw near to each of us and help us find our comfort and support in You. Show us how to be lights in this dark world to those we love but who do not know Your forgiveness and salvation. Let us bring comfort to these dear ones through both word and deed.

Make Your presence known every hour, I pray. Help me to see the good even in this hard, hard place. Open our eyes to see Your new-morning mercies and to look for the good every day. Lord, thank You for being with us. I know that Your Word is true when it says we can do hard things because God is with us. Let that truth become a reality for all of us today. Amen.

Fighting for Joy

1. *Find joy in God's past faithfulness.* Take a look back and begin your day by thanking God for His past presence and loving faithfulness toward you. Then ask God to open your eyes to today's new-morning mercies. Ask Him to show you the good even in the hard today. As you reflect upon God's compassion and care in the past, remind yourself that His promises never alter or change and that He is the same God, always and forever.

2. *Find joy in God's present faithfulness.* Before getting busy in your day, prioritize time spent alone in God's presence. Open your Bible and select at least five psalms to slowly read and then meditate upon. As you read and silently meditate on these comforting truths about God's perfect care and nearness in suffering, thank Him for His faithful compassionate care for you. Carry one of these verses with you to reread and reflect upon when you begin to feel overwhelmed by your suffering and sorrow.
3. *Find joy in God's future faithfulness.* As you end your day, spend time with God in quiet contemplation. Pray about specific issues with which you are struggling. Ask God to oversee each problem, to heal every sorrow, and to bring renewed hope and joy back into your heart. By faith, end your day by thanking God in advance for the good He will accomplish, even out of these hard times. And thank Him, too, for giving you eyes to see the good even in the hard. Praise Him for His intimate and intense love for you every day.

28

Trust in the Steadfast Love of God

Before a word is on my tongue
you, Lord, know it completely.

Psalm 139:4

A GOOD FRIEND of mine is experiencing a lot of ups and downs these days. Both her mother and her mother-in-law have dementia. Each time she visits these dear women she witnesses their advancing mental decline. It hurts so much, she tells me, to attempt to have a normal conversation with those closest to you when they can no longer understand and process daily conversation. Heartbreaking.

I've listened to my friend describe her sorrow as she observes these two women of God lose their memories, their cognitive abilities, and their joy. They are both keenly aware that they cannot think as they once did—and it grieves them. Try as their families might, nothing seems to soothe these aged believers when they attempt to communicate as they once did cannot. Heartbreaking.

While no easy answers exist for this painful situation, and no one can cure them or turn back the hands of time, my friend has recently discovered that when she spends time with her mother and her mother-in-law her own joy can stir a joyous response in them.

I've watched it happen. For a long while, my friend felt so grieved by their impairment that it showed in her face. In her eyes. In her posture. Her grief was up front. And though her own mother and mother-in-law might not know the cause, they were aware of their daughter's and daughter-in-law's heartache.

Over a period of months during which my friend felt increasingly sad by what may come next, something significant changed. While reading through Psalm 139, she discovered a wondrous biblical truth that she had previously passed over.

It was this: God knows. He knows. And He does. This verse, Psalm 139:4, says, "Before a word is on my tongue / you, Lord, know it completely." My dear friend suddenly had a light bulb moment of the supernatural variety. She was comforted by the amazing statement that God knows.

Before we even utter a word, He knows. Before our beloved aged family members utter a word, which often doesn't make sense, He knows. He knows. God always knows.

As our Creator and our beloved heavenly Father, our God knows. As we read through Psalm 139, we can discover or rediscover the wonder and beauty of being perfectly conceived, perfectly loved, and perfectly known. Is there a better gift than that?

My friend who is watching two of the most important women in her life decline is comforted by the fact that God knows what they are going through. He knows.

My friend's mother and mother-in-law can be comforted by the fact that their beloved Savior knows, too. God knows. He knows. God knows what and how they are trying to communicate. He knows their failing bodies and minds. He knows their fears, their worries, and their emotional lows. He knows.

Once my friend experienced her "Ah-hah!" moment, everything changed. Nothing changed in her mother's and mother-in-law's dementia, but her attitude toward their decline did.

Today, my friend doesn't expect either of these women to recall recent events. She does expect to spend quality time with them, both telling them about long-ago shared experiences that they do remember. She tells jokes. She explains (again and again) simple tasks. She makes them smile. She smiles herself—and their joy is increasing.

Perhaps the most telling practical step my friend has taken since her "Ah-hah!" moment is this: now she enters into conversations with a purposeful and expectant heart because she eagerly tells them about Jesus. She speaks of His love, His forgiveness, His care, and His promise to walk with them until they see Him face to face.

Joy isn't always produced by the words we speak to others. It can be the outpouring of a joyous spirit that evidences itself in our faces, our eyes, and our postures. May we all seek to infuse others with joy everlasting!

My Heart's Cry

Father, I simultaneously feel both joy and sorrow as I watch my dear ones decline in so many ways. Please help me to keep my eyes focused on You alone, not on hard circumstances. I know that I cannot change this situation but I believe You want me to be a joy infuser in my loved ones' lives.

Give me Your smile today. Give me Your joy abundant. Show me how to lighten their suffering with compassion and care. Help me to view their present suffering in light of eternity confident that You know.

Thank You, Lord, for overseeing every step we take, every thought we ponder, every word we speak. You are the God who knows, who sees and who cares. Amen.

Fighting for Joy

1. *Find joy in God's past faithfulness.* As you seek to find joy in today's suffering and hard circumstances, be a good rememberer. Recall what God has done in your past. Remember that He is always present and that He always knows. Take comfort in all the ways that God showed His perfect love for you in days gone by and give Him thanks.
2. *Find joy in God's present faithfulness.* Present your petitions to God today with a heart that is sensitive to God's promise that He knows. God knows. He knows what you are enduring. He knows what you are feeling. He knows what you desire to change. He knows. Be comforted by God's present and perfect plan for you and those you love.
3. *Find joy in God's future faithfulness.* As you reflect on your day, ask the Lord to help you reframe even the most sorrowful moments as you think on His promises. Take comfort in God as you mentally survey the unknown future. Ask the Lord to bring you that peace beyond measure in spite of the difficulties and discouragements you face. Then remember to rejoice in God and His everlasting love for you and those whom you love.

29

Find Joy in Ordinary Days

He has told you, O man, what is good; and what does the LORD require of you but to do justice, and to love kindness, and to walk humbly with your God?

Micah 6:8, ESV

I LOVE THE words of author and biblical counselor Paul Tripp who said, "Most of our big life's decisions can be counted on one hand."

It's true. Tripp explains that most of us decide on higher education (or not); decide to pursue a specific vocation (or not); decide to marry (or not); decide where to live (or not to live); etc. Our biggest life decisions truly are few and far between. However, we make up for these large decisions by the countless small choices we make minute by minute.

One of the most common misconceptions about life is that it will be filled with momentous days. But in a large part, our lives are filled with ordinary, nondescript days. And to be honest, wouldn't we all rather have more of what we term "ordinary days?" I surely would.

Many years ago, I read about Elizabeth Elliot's husband's fight with cancer and she wrote: "How we longed for a simple ordinary day when he wasn't fighting against pain and suffering."

From her perspective the ordinary far and away eclipsed the spectacular. If we're wise, the ordinary days that God bestows can be some of the finest days of our lives. But in order for us to appreciate and fully value our ordinary lives; we have to have eyes to see.

Along this same vein, we must learn to take note of God's common grace. God's goodness is to all He has created. That means that everyone (believer or not) can observe and appreciate God's created world with all its blessings. We can see the beauty of nature in all its stunning glory. We can see God's intricate handiwork by how He has designed flora and fauna, as well as every species of animal. We can see His nature revealed when we take the time and notice the diversity of every human He has planned before the dawn of time.

As we learn to foster humility and contentment in our ordinary days, we will see our joy flourish. We won't be held captive by the suffering and pain surrounding us. Rather, with God's enabling grace, we can transcend the grief, and it can be transformed into abundant joy. Yet once again, this is where we must choose to fight for joy. Discovering the wonder and joy of ordinary days when nothing much is happening—or conversely when a lot is happening—we can find our joy complete.

Our task then can be described in this passage of Micah where the writer tells us to act with justice, to love kindness, and to walk humbly with our God. All these elements speak of a trusting, intimate relationship with our beloved heavenly Father, who is carefully overseeing our entire lives in both the mundane and the magnificent.

As we reflect upon the days of our lives, we must choose to fight for joy. It won't come easy. It won't suddenly overshadow our pain and suffering unless we decide to battle for it. But how does this work exactly? As this Scripture states, we need to seek what is good. We must live justly and love kindness. And perhaps the overarching capstone may be that we learn to walk humbly with our God as we submit to His sovereign rule no matter the cost. We can find joy in our ordinary days if only we have eyes to see.

My Heart's Cry

Father, today I am fighting for joy again. It seems as though I'm even battling to place one foot in front of the other. My hours and days are filled with setbacks and difficulty. Oh how I long for a single ordinary day when nothing of much import is happening. Help me, Lord, to be content in whatever You deem best for me today. Give me Your grace and strength to fulfill my responsibilities with a thankful, humble heart. Show me Your goodness everywhere I set my eyes. Open my heart to receive Your joy in all its abundance. Amen.

Fighting for Joy

1. *Find joy in God's past faithfulness.* If you are facing an ordinary day, spend some time alone with God in prayer and thanksgiving. Ask Him to give you eyes to see the common grace He has blessed and bestowed upon all He has made. Then take a few moments to offer praise and worship for all the goodness you observe from His kind and compassionate hand.
2. *Find joy in God's present faithfulness.* Worship the Lord in gladness today as you open your heart and mind to His blessings, which surround you. One by one, thank God for His bountiful and generous love toward you in these blessings. Ask Him to renew and restore your joy, if it has been found waning. Pray for the eyes to see the glory of ordinary days and give thanks for each one.

3. *Find joy in God's future faithfulness.* As you contemplate your tomorrows, resist giving way to worry or concern because of the unknowns. Place the full weight of your hope and trust in the goodness of God. Remind yourself of His past and present faithfulnesses to you. Ask Him to bring to your remembrance all the small and large evidences of His extravagant love toward you. Then take time to sit in silence before Him and worship God for the wonder and grandeur of the created world and all that He has placed in it for our enjoyment and pleasure.

30

Praise God for His Tender Mercies

Surely goodness and mercy shall follow me all the days of my life, and I shall dwell in the house of the LORD forever.

Psalm 23:6, ESV

HAVE YOU EVER considered that having too much mercy is not a good thing? Until recently, I would have vehemently disagreed with this statement. Then I read through the Psalms and Proverbs and noticed how often God transforms us and our situations that use suffering to accomplish His sanctification process and bring Him glory.

Sometimes we hold onto the suffering of those we love because we feel so badly for their plight that we stop trusting that God knows best. Worse yet, we begin to believe that we know better than God how to rule and govern the lives of those we love.

It's not uncommon for us to struggle spiritually as we observe others in the throes of pain. It does hurt us when we watch others hurt. God knows this, but I believe He wants us to press closer in to Him and pour our troubled hearts out to Him. He promises to meet us there, in prayer.

However, our faith in God's sovereignty must override our vacillating emotions. We must remember God's loving rebuke to Job as He reminded Job of the worlds He had created and how He maintained life on earth and in the heavens by the Word of His power. It is so easy to fall into the trap of judging God and how He has chosen to govern His world.

Another faulty trap we frequently fall into is that when we nurture mercy to the point that we stop trusting God, and we often forfeit our joy as well. In fact, we question God's way of governing the world, which indicates our lack of trust, lack of faith, and lack of confidence in His unchanging character as revealed throughout Scripture.

At this critical juncture, we need to confess our sin and ask God to give us the wisdom, insight, and understanding we require to face our—and others'—hardships with a robust faith that never wavers.

When we learn to trust our heavenly Father with all the hard things in our lives, even our suffering pales in comparison to the genuine peace we can experience within our hearts and minds. As we choose to look to God with the eyes of faith and trust regardless of what is happening to us or around us, God promises that mercy and goodness will follow us all the days of our lives. And what better ending to this powerful promise than this: "And [we] shall dwell in the house of the LORD forever."

As we make the hard choice to stop trying to figure out why God allows the suffering He has ordained, and we choose to trust in His loving and compassionate care, we will discover a wealth of spiritual blessings.

Our hearts will learn to reframe even the most heartbreaking of life's scenarios into those God will use to transform us into the image of Jesus. The more we learn to value holiness the more easily we will learn to accept the suffering God allows to touch us.

Only when we truly understand who God is as Scripture depicts Him throughout the Old and New Testament will we find our safety and security within the confines of His loving plan for our lives. Only when we choose to accept what God has given will we rest soundly, no matter what transpires in the coming days.

As we lean hard into the loving arms of Christ, we will find all that we need to experience peace, love, and joy abundantly. Yes, our fight for joy is one we must choose to pursue with all the spiritual resources we have. God's Word tells us that goodness and mercy shall follow us all the days of our lives and we will dwell in the house of the Lord forever. What a joyous thought. What a joy-filled promise! What a God we serve!

My Heart's Cry

Father, I feel so burdened by that pain my dear ones endure right now. I want nothing more than to stop their suffering. But I cannot. I dare not. I know that You are sovereign over all of creation, and I must pour my heart to You and learn to trust You more fully. But I feel so weary and weak.

Help me, Lord, to lean in hard and learn to rest in Your loving presence. Give me Your divine wisdom, insight, and understanding to see past the pain and to what You can accomplish through it. Open my eyes, and let me see Your goodness and Your mercy every day. Fill my heart with joy that never wavers. Amen.

Fighting for Joy

1. *Find joy in God's past faithfulness.* In the morning, spend some quiet moments giving thanks to God for His past mercy and goodness upon your life. Think back to moments when the pain you felt or the mercy you experienced for others was all-consuming. Then remember what God has done. Thank Him for His perfect provision in times of suffering and sorrow. Praise Him for unwavering love He has set upon you.
2. *Find joy in God's present faithfulness.* Ask God to open your eyes to see the goodness and mercy He is filling your life with today. Even in the midst of difficulties and hardship, by faith, thank God for the good He will bring out of these hard times. Pray that God will bolster your faith and renew your joy even as you wait for this sorrow to pass. Then spend a few moments in silence contemplating the verse, "Be still and know that I am God" (Ps. 46:10).
3. *Find joy in God's future faithfulness.* Praise God for the goodness and mercy He has promised to fill your life with day by day. Give thanks to God for His tender mercies toward you even when you feel depleted by life's hardships. Give thanks to God that at the end of the day His promise for us to dwell in the house of the Lord will stand forever. Give thanks to God for He is good, and all that He does is good.

This book is published by CLC Publications, an outreach of CLC Ministries International. The purpose of CLC is to make evangelical Christian literature available to all nations so people may come to faith and maturity in the Lord Jesus Christ. We hope this book has been life changing and has enriched your walk with God through the work of the Holy Spirit. If you would like to know more about CLC, we invite you to visit our website:

www.clcusa.org

To know more about the remarkable story of the founding of CLC International we encourage you to read

LEAP OF FAITH

Norman Grubb

PRAISE!

A DOOR TO GOD'S PRESENCE

"I will extol the LORD at all times;
his praise will always be on my lips."

(Psalm 34:1)

Do you practice praising God? God deserves all our praise! But what is the importance of praise in the life of a Christian? How can praise deepen our relationship with God? What does godly, biblical, and God-honoring praise look like? What does Scripture say about praise?

Warren and Ruth Myers call on all Christians to cultivate a deeper relationship with God through the daily practice of rich praise.

Warren and Ruth showcase the biblical foundation for praise and invite you to enter the true joy and freedom of praising our glorious God.

Discover how to praise the Lord in spirit and truth in ***Praise!***

Includes a one-week devotional study on praise

Size $5^{1}/_{4}$ x 8, Pages 185
ISBN: 978-1-61958-386-3
ISBN (*e-book*): 978-1-61958-389-4

PRAY!

HOW TO BE EFFECTIVE IN PRAYER

"Lord, teach us to pray."

(Luke 11:1)

God loves when His people pray! But just how important is prayer in the life of a Christian? What should we pray about? Does God care how often we pray or what we pray for?

In this book, Warren and Ruth Myers teach us how to pray, outlining the biblical principles, patterns, and practices of prayer. They offer a rich theology of prayer, but also provide practical ways to enrich your prayer life. Whether shaping habits for your own quiet time or explaining the Lord's Prayer, Warren and Ruth use Scripture as the foundation for their teaching. They exhort all Christians to practice prayer, dependent on the help of the Holy Spirit, to intercede for the lost and support God's global mission.

Learn how to pray, whom to pray for, and why prayer matters.

Includes prayer-based tips for planning your quiet time

Size 5¼ x 8, Pages 211
ISBN: 978-1-61958-387-0
ISBN (*e-book*): 978-1-61958-388-7

DAILY THOUGHTS ON HOLINESS

Andrew Murray

This compilation of daily devotional readings emphasizes the focuses of Andrew Murray's writing and preaching—holiness and the deepening of the spiritual life. These bite-sized reflections will lead you in a day-to-day development of a holy life.

Paperback
Size $4^1/_4$ x 7, Pages 374
ISBN: 978-1-936143-48-1
IBSN (*e-book*): 978-1-61958-015-2